Information Systems and Computer Applications

CLEP* Test Study Guide

All rights reserved. This Study Guide, Book and Flashcards are protected under the US Copyright Law. No part of this book or study guide or flashcards may be reproduced, distributed or stored in a retrieval system, or transmitted in any form or by any means, electronic, mechanical, photocopying, recording, or otherwise, without the prior written permission of the publisher Breely Crush Publishing, LLC.

© 2026 Breely Crush Publishing, LLC

*CLEP is a registered trademark of the College Entrance Examination Board which does not endorse this book.

971052024143

Copyright ©2003 - 2026, Breely Crush Publishing, LLC.

All rights reserved.

This Study Guide, Book and Flashcards are protected under the US Copyright Law. No part of this publication may be reproduced, distributed or stored in a retrieval system, or transmitted in any form or by any means, electronic, mechanical, photocopying, recording, or otherwise, without the prior written permission of the publisher Breely Crush Publishing, LLC.

Published by Breely Crush Publishing, LLC
10808 River Front Parkway
South Jordan, UT 84095
www.breelycrushpublishing.com

ISBN-13: 978-1-61433-639-6

Printed and bound in the United States of America.

*CLEP is a registered trademark of the College Entrance Examination Board which does not endorse this book.

Table of Contents

Computer Hardware and Functions *1*
    Computer Configurations *2*
    Computer Devices *2*
Digital Representation *5*
Networks *6*
Relevance to Business *9*
Network and Client/Server Architectures *13*
    Local Area Network *13*
    Wide Area Network *16*
    Network Cabling *16*
    Communications Protocol *17*
    Modem and Fax *18*
Operating Systems *18*
Software Development Methods and Tools *21*
    Methods *21*
    Tools *22*
    Pseudocode *24*
    Conversion to a New System *27*
Programming Languages *27*
    What is the Difference Between a Compiler and an Interpreter? *28*
    Categories of High Level Languages *28*
User Interfaces *31*
Software Packages *32*
Data Management *33*
    Data Concepts and Data Structures *33*
    Database Management Systems *34*
    Hypertext and Hypermedia *35*
    Document Images *36*
Data Models *37*
Hierarchy of Data *41*
Organizing Data *41*
Data Query *42*
Data Update *42*
DBMS *43*
Information Processing Management *44*
    System Development Processes *44*
    Types of Information Processing Applications *45*
    Standards *45*
Security and Controls *46*

Information Processing Careers	*47*
Applications in Organizations	*48*
Management Decision Making	*48*
User Applications	*49*
Office Systems	*51*
Internet and the World Wide Web	*51*
Social and Ethical Issues	*53*
Software Licensing	*55*
Safety and Security for Networks	*55*
Mobile Networks	*56*
Satellite Transmissions	*56*
Software Life Cycle	*57*
Programming Methodology	*59*
Data Types and Algorithms	*59*
Programming Concepts	*61*
Logic Concepts	*62*
Software Development Tools	*64*
Sample Test Questions	*66*
Test Taking Strategies	*99*
What Your Score Means	*100*
Test Preparation	*100*
Legal Note	*101*

 Computer Hardware and Functions

The term computer hardware refers to any of the electronic components that make up the computer, such as the monitor, the CPU, the disk drives, or the printer. Hardware is separate from software, the general term for any program that performs calculations and controls what you see on the monitor. A computer comes with some basic software when it is purchased; this software is known as the operating system. An operating system (OS) is a master control program that oversees all computer functions and manages how information is placed onto the various hardware devices. Microsoft Windows is an example of a popular operating system.

The computer's CPU, also known as the central processing unit, is the primary microprocessor that governs the computer's operations. Most personal computers (PC's) rely on microprocessors manufactured by Intel, such as the Pentium or Celeron processor. The CPU's speed directly impacts the performance of software programs. The CPU comprises three essential components: an arithmetic logic unit, a control unit, and a set of registers.

The CPU, or Central Processing Unit, is famed for being the "brain" of the computer. It is a small piece on the inside of the computer which is essentially responsible for running the whole computer. It processes the information and instructions given to it by programs to allow computer users to do anything from writing papers to playing games. Everything that the computer does goes through the CPU, making it a very important element. The CPU has four main functions. They are fetch, decode, execute, and writeback.

Fetch describes the CPU's search for the information it needs. Sometimes, it searches through the RAM, program memory, or hard drive. As the CPU goes through a step-by-step process, it must fetch the information it needs for each step.

Once the CPU has fetched the information, it must decode it. The language computerwork in is binary code, a series of 0s and 1s. Different languages have been developed because writing programs in binary code would take so much time and effort. The computer has to translate programs into binary code because they are written in these different languages. This is done through the use of compilers.

Based on the instructions which have been decoded, the CPU can then execute the instructions. For example, a person types 24/6 into their computer's built-in calculator function. This command goes to the CPU (the fetch stage). It is then translated into binary code which the CPU understands (the decode stage). It recognizes that division is needed to solve the problem and uses preprogrammed division logic to come up with the answer: four.

Having the answer, it moves to the last step, writeback. In the writeback stage the CPU produces output. In this case, the output is displaying the number four, but depending on the command it was given, the output could be any number of things. Once the CPU has finished the cycle, it starts again with another task or step.

Pipelining refers to a CPU's ability to process more than one task at a time. The pipeline will divide into segments, with each designated a different task. One will fetch and pass it on to the next, and fetch again, while their other segments work on it. This way the CPU works faster and more efficiently.

Every computer has an **instruction set**, which is a list of keywords that corresponds to all of the operations that the CPU contains. CPU's can be a **complex instruction set computer (CISC)** that support approximately 100 instructions for greater speed or a **reduced instruction set computer (RISC)** with a minimal set of instructions designed for a specialized application.

Registers are specialized storage areas that store values while the instructions operate upon them. The **arithmetic logic unit (ALU)** is the component of the CPU that supports the standard arithmetic functions like add and subtract as well as logical operations like AND and OR. The **control unit** is the electronic controller over the operations that the instructions perform much like the brain controls our actions.

COMPUTER CONFIGURATIONS

A personal computer (PC) is a small computer equipped with its own operating system and peripheral devices typically needed by one individual. PCs are differentiated from a personal digital assistant (PDA), which is a hand-held computer customized for everyday functions for personal organization, such as an appointment calendar, an address book, a notepad, and fax or other two-way messaging capability.

Large companies historically have relied upon some form of mainframe computer to handle their voluminous data processing needs. A mainframe computer is a multi-user computer capable of simultaneously processing thousands of calculations. Mainframe computers were the primary type of computers available from the 1960s onward.

COMPUTER DEVICES

Another critical hardware device is the hard disk or disk drive. The hard disk is an electronic component of the computer that is used for storing information. It may also be called a hard drive. The hard disk offers RAM, which means data can be read from and written to this device. RAM is distinguished from ROM memory found in the CPU; ROM memory is read-only. It makes sense that parts of the operating system are read-only; that is, nothing else can be written over the basics of the operating system. The computer will no longer operate properly if the operating system is destroyed. Volatile memory is any type of memory that is erased when the computer is turned off. For example, RAM empties when the computer is turned off. This is why files must be saved on a hard drive or to another permanent memory device. However, this doesn't make the RAM useless – it is very helpful in speeding up computer functions.

A cache is a small memory unit used by the CPU. Level 1 cache, or L1 cache, is generally built into the CPU, and the level 2, or L2 cache, is generally attached to the motherboard. The caches store information about programs. When the request for the information comes up, the CPU can find it much faster than if it had to search the RAM or hard drive. The CPU first searches the L1 cache, then the L2 cache, and if it isn't in either place, it will proceed to the RAM. Multiple small caches are used instead of one large cache because the smaller they are, the faster the CPU can search them.

The hard disk is an integral part of the computer and is portable only to the extent that the computer itself is portable, such as a notebook or laptop PC. Alternate drives are available to handle portable information storage devices such as floppy disks, diskettes, or CDs. Floppy disks are 5.25-inch portable storage devices that are mostly out-of-date today, while diskettes are 3.5 inches wide and encased in plastic. Neither of these is typically used anymore.

CDs or compact disks replaced disks as the latest in portable information devices. These were soon replaced by DVDs, which can hold much more data. Blu-ray is a new type of disc with a higher storage capacity than CDs or DVDs, which makes it useful for high-definition videos. Part of the reason it is able to do this is because while regular DVDs are read using a red laser, Blu-ray discs are read with a blue laser. Blue lasers have a shorter wavelength than red lasers and can read more closely packed information.

All storage devices can be divided into files, which represent individual documents or other collections of information identified by unique names.

The computer user communicates with the software and CPU by entering information through a keyboard, which is called an input device because it is used to enter information into the computer. The keyboard provides alphabetic, numeric, punctuation, symbols, and control keys. When a key is depressed, an electronic signal that is unique to the key is sent to the CPU.

The operating system typically displays the associated letter, number, or symbol on the monitor, a piece of hardware resembling a television screen. Monitors use screen resolution, also called display resolution, to describe the clarity of a screen. Screen resolution is defined in terms of pixels. A pixel is a specific point on the screen. Therefore, the more pixels, the higher the quality of the images will be.

The refresh rate, or vertical refresh rate, describes the number of times per second that a computer screen is redrawn or updated. It is measured in hertz (Hz). Typically, a refresh rate lower than 60 Hz will have a noticeable flicker. However, as refresh rates increase, this does not always produce a noticeable difference.

The computer user also enters information by using a communication device known as a mouse. A mouse is another input device. This device fits easily in the human hand and is designed to roll on a flat surface that roughly translates to the monitor's area. The mouse is used to locate an area the user is interested in on the monitor. Clicking the buttons on the mouse is a typical method for selecting options that are displayed on the monitor by software programs.

The keyboard, monitor and mouse are the primary peripheral devices that are used for entering information into the computer. A **peripheral device** is any electronic component that is attached to the computer but external to it. Another external peripheral device is a **scanner**, which is used to copy paper documents or pictures into memory on the hard drive. A touch screen is another input device that is used in applications that are available to a general user. The **touch screen** enters the user's choices based upon a simple pressing of the indicated area of the pressure-sensitive panel.

Bar code readers are used in business applications to interpret bar codes that indicate what the product is, and they are particularly important in warehousing applications. A **point-of-sale (POS) terminal** is a computerized cash register that allows the input of data such as item sold, price, and method of payment.

Digital cameras can now be connected directly to a personal computer for downloading pictures onto the hard disk. Most also have the option of removing additional storage via a memory card which can be inserted into a card reader to access the information. Most PCs now come equipped with media card readers included. A scanner is an input device. It is used to get an image from paper to the computer screen.

Just as there are a variety of peripheral devices for input, there are also numerous **output devices,** that is, components whose main purpose is to retrieve processed information that is stored in the computer's memory. The most familiar output device is a **printer**, which produces a paper copy of the desired document, picture, or graphs. Some printers are now special purpose devices that are designed only to print pictures. The computer **monitor** serves as an output device when it is used to retrieve information that is stored in memory. The **PC speakers** are also an output device for audio messages that accompany software systems or that are recorded on Internet web sites.

Printers, fax machines and scanners are different input and output devices used in transferring data to and from computers. A printer is an output machine. It is linked to the computer and reproduces images on paper in either color or black and white. A fax machine processes input, such as text, and sends it over a phone line to another computer.

Digital Representation

Computers are electronic and can only store information as a group of binary digits that is composed of 0's and 1's only. Each binary digit is known as a bit. Eight consecutive bits in computer memory are called a byte.

Our normal arithmetic is base 10 or decimal, with digits 0-9 only. Binary arithmetic within the computer is base 2, with digits 0-1 only. So decimal 0 is 0 binary, 1 is 1, but 2 is 10 binary, and 3 is 11 binary, 4 is 100 binary and so on. While the internal computer performs numeric calculations in binary, the operating system converts the internal binary to the decimal system we are accustomed to whenever the numbers are sent to an output device such as the monitor or printer. Sometimes, very large numbers are stored in the computer in a form known as binary-coded decimal (BCD), where each decimal digit is stored as a 4-bit binary number.

How are letters or text stored? The letters that come in as electronic signals from the keyboard are converted to Extended Binary Coded Decimal Interchange Code (EBCDIC) for IBM mainframe computers and American Standard Code for Information Interchange (ASCII) for personal computers. The basic idea for these codes is that every letter of the alphabet and every other symbol, like the punctuation marks and percent sign, are converted to a binary code that fits into an 8-bit byte; however, ASCII coding uses only 7 of the 8 bits. These byte-oriented encoding schemes can handle 256 possible characters and symbols and thus are not suited for languages that have more symbols, like some of the Oriental languages.

Pictures have their own graphics digital representation or Joint Photographic Experts Group (JPEG) format. This format can represent up to 16.7 million color variations for each pixel or picture element. JPEG images are best used in the case of photographs or other images which require smooth color transitions and patterns. They are often used as the files created when you take a picture with a digital camera. JPEGs are also useful for Internet purposes because they can compress well.

GIF images are used for images with sharp contrast between colors, such as with animations or logos. They can also be used as short, low resolution video clips.

PNG files were actually designed to replace GIFs. They do not, however, support animations. They do have a larger color range than GIFs do, and they are better with gradual color changes.

A pixel is the smallest picture element that an output device can handle. A pixel is the smallest identifiable element on a computer screen. Essentially, what is seen on a computer screen is the result of millions of pixels being manipulated to create a display. The resolution, or clarity, of the screen is determined by the amount of pixels there are. The more pixels there are, the higher the resolution is. The higher the resolution is, the sharper the image. For example, a computer with resolution 1360 x 900 would have over 1.2 million pixels, 1,224,000 pixels to be exact. However, a computer with 640 x 480 resolution would have only 307,000 total pixels.

A picture is composed of a grid of pixels. Another picture format is **Tagged Image File Format (TIFF)** that is used for scanned photographic images. Graphs and graphics files are compressed using **Graphics Interchange Format (GIF)**. Video has its own format as well, namely the **Moving Picture Experts Group (MPEG)** format which provides for the compression of digitized videos and animation. **Vector Graphics** are images generated from mathematical descriptions of where line length, positioning and other shapes should be. Raster graphics programs produce **bitmaps (BMP)** which are details of each row and column of pixel.

MPEG files are higher quality digital videos.

MP3 files are audio files.

Audio files are often put into this file format to be transferred from one computer (or device) to another.

BIF files are Boot Information Files. They are used to boot a computer from a disc. DOC files, or documents, are word processing files.

Networks

A computer network may involve as few as three computers. The internet is a network of millions of computers and servers. Each computer within a network is called a node.

Networks come in many configurations:
- **Mesh:** Every computer in the network is linked to every other computer.
- **Star:** There is a central computer. Every other computer in the network is linked to the central computer.
- **Hierarchy:** One node is linked to several child nodes. Each of these is the parent to another level of nodes.
- **Bus:** Each computer is linked linearly to a single communication channel ("bus").
- **Ring:** Computers are linked circularly to a single communication channel.

Hybrid: Networks are linked in a combination of two or more structures.

SUMMARY OF NETWORK CONFIGURATIONS		
Structure	*Advantage*	*Disadvantage*
Mesh	Quick and efficient data transmission	Adding new nodes difficult
Star	Data travels only a short distance	Entire network down if central computer fails
Hierarchy	More reliable, as network can survive if a lower level node fails	Data must travel longer distance, therefore slower data flow
Bus	Reliable, network very resilient if any computer fails	Very slow data flow
Ring	Reliable, as in a bus configuration	Slow

Network designs work on a continuum of reliability and speed. The most reliable configurations are usually the slowest. Hybrid systems try to maximize the benefits of two or more designs.

Networks may be divided into two general types based on their size. A **local area network (LAN)** covers a small geographic area, for example a hospital campus or an office building. **Wide area networks (WANs)** cover large geographic areas, for example a city or several countries. **Internetworks** are comprised of connected LANs and WANs.

Local Area Networks

LANs can be wired or wireless. They are usually ring or bus networks and require specialized hardware and software. A network interface card (NIC) connects a computer to the communications channel. Applications are needed to allow the node to send and receive information across the network.

A LAN may include resource servers that can be accessed by the client computers:

>**Print server:** Allows every computer connected to the server to share the printer.
>**File server:** Allows connected computers to share a secondary storage device.
>**Database server:** Server connected to a secondary storage device used in database processing throughout the LAN.

Wide Area Networks and Internetworks

WANs may be star, hierarchical or hybrid configurations and may include many types of computers. Internetworks are used to connect individual LANs and WANs. Connections between similar networks, such as two LANs, are achieved through a **bridge**. Two different networks, a LAN and a WAN for instance, are linked with a **gateway**. A **router** is used to direct messages to the correct destinations throughout the connected networks.

The **internet** is a public internetwork which contains a collection of web pages, each identified by a unique uniform resource locator (URL). The internet has become so popular, that many organizations use an **intranet**, which is a network based on the internet but limited to internal users.

In addition to classifications of networks, there are also many elements within a network that require explanation. Although some networks connect through token ring topology, in which devices are connected in a circle, many topologies connect through hubs. The computers and other devices are all connected directly to the hub, and thereby indirectly connected to each other. Switches perform a similar function as hubs in that they can be used to connect computers in a network. However, they can generate increased productivity because they allow for two way communication, meaning that messages can be sent and received at the same time. Another advantage over hubs is that switches allow data to be transferred directly between two computers, rather than broadcasted over an entire network.

Routers and firewalls are used to regulate the connections between networks. Routers establish a connection between networks and then regulate the traffic over that connection. One common use of a router is to connect a school or office network to the internet (which is a network itself). The router transmits data between the two, and can deny access where necessary. A firewall is a device which prevents unauthorized access to a network. Because routers can deny access to a network they function as one type of firewall, but the classification includes many additional functions. Firewalls are specifically created to protect a network, and screen all of the data, either sent or received, that passes through it.

Relevance to Business

LANs

LANs can be an effective and efficient way for users throughout an organization to share information and resources. Client/server systems, where data is stored in a centralized database on the server then sent to client computers as users require it, are often preferred over multiple-user computer systems for many reasons:

- In client/server environments, the server does not handle the data processing, database management or user interface. This allows the organization to buy a smaller computer to act as a server than would be required for the central computer of a comparable multiple-user system.
- It is cheaper and easier to add new client computers as the company grows than to it is to add additional multiple-user computers.

WANs

WANs are often preferred by businesses that have operations separated by long distances. WANS may be based on public or private communication networks. Depending on the size of the area that needs to be connected, businesses may purchase their own cables or wireless system, or they can lease long-distance channels – usually the more economical choice for networks that span very large areas.

Businesses may choose to purchase the hardware and software required to connect to a WAN, or they may contract long-distance links and value-added networks with a communications company. A value-added network (VAN) includes additional software and hardware the company may find useful.

Businesses may choose to use the internet instead of a common carrier channel or VAN. In this case, security measures such as data encryption and user authentication may be needed to protect company information and correspondence.

Electronic Commerce

Organizations often use networks to facilitate electronic commerce (e-commerce). Ecommerce involves a **web server**, which stores the pages of the business's website and is equipped with specialized software. An organization may use its own web server or one provided by an internet service provider (ISP).

A web server is often linked to a database server by a LAN. The database server contains information necessary for e-commerce, for example product availability and prices. A customer initiates an e-commerce transaction by accessing the business's website. When a customer places an order, the web server uses information from the database server to process orders. The order information is sent back to the customer.

Security

Organizations need to keep their information secure while it is being stored ("at rest"), and when it is being transferred across a network ("in motion"). Federal, state, local and industrial regulations set standards for adequate security. Organizations that are not compliant with these ordinances may face legal sanctions and fines.

Records that should be protected includes information about customers, employees and business processes. In addition, organizations often want to protect their financial records, business processes, marketing strategies and future plans.

Information security breaches can be the result of either malicious or nonmalicious attacks. Malicious attacks, those that are intended to gain access to or harm secure information, may be the work of hacking, disgruntled employees, organized crime or espionage. Nonmalicious attacks are often caused by careless employees and poorly trained system users.

There are five classes of attacks identified by the National Security Agency:

- **Passive attacks** include capturing passwords or other data by monitoring communications.
- **Active attacks** cause corrupted files, denial of service or information disclosure by overriding security systems or introducing malicious programs.
- **Close-in attacks** require the physical presence of the attacker to access information or to corrupt files.
- **Insider attacks** are those by people within the organization.

- **Distribution attacks** are malicious changes in the system hardware or software during distribution or construction. For example, a programmer may leave a "back door" in an application to allow future access to the system.

Organizations attempt to protect themselves from attacks by using physical, administrative and technological safeguards.

Physical Security

Most security breaches can be prevented by adequate physical safeguards. Physical security attempts to prevent the theft and loss of hardware and storage media. Some physical security measures include:

- limited offsite transport of equipment and disks
- secure disposal of retired equipment
- monitored use of equipment

Administrative Security

Administrative safeguards include written policies and procedures addressing issues such as:

- what to do if a data breach is suspected
- security training
- who may have access to what data
- current and future protection needs
- sanctions if security policies are broken by employees

Technological Security

Technological security includes hardware and software used to keep in motion and at rest data safe. These measures may include:

- password systems
- two-way handshakes
- three-way handshakes
- digital signatures
- centralized logging
- external authentication

Password systems

Password systems require users to log in before using selected applications or accessing data. An intercepted password, or a password that has been discovered through a brute force method, make the system vulnerable to access by unauthorized users. In a **brute**

force attack, malicious attackers attempt to discover a password by trying all possible combinations.

Organizations can make password systems more effective by:

- Requiring each user to have a unique username and related password. This also allows for better tracking of who is accessing what information.
- Requiring passwords to be longer than a certain number of characters and to contain numbers, letter and symbols. This increases the number of possible passwords, therefore decreasing the likelihood of a brute force attack finding a password.
- Automatically logging users out when the session becomes inactive.
- Randomly assigning passwords or requiring periodic password changes. Users may be relying on the same password for multiple systems. If one password is intercepted, multiple systems may be vulnerable.
- Using encryption whenever passwords are transmitted across the network.

Handshakes

Handshakes are the exchange of information between different elements of a system in order to confirm authorization before accessing and transmitting information.

In a two-way handshake, the equipment or application requesting data sends an electronic code. Another code is sent by the system element from which data is being requested. Before any information is transmitted, both codes are verified. A three-way handshake requires another verified code from the requestor before data can be transmitted.

Digital signatures

Digital signatures authenticate data transfers through the use of mathematical algorithms. The transmitting element in the system signs the data transfer using a secret formula, the "private key." The receiving element verifies that the signature is authentic using an open "public" key. Digital signatures can be used to verify that changes to data files are from authorized users. This can help maintain the integrity of an information system.

Centralized logging

Centralized logging involves the recording of every entry to, access of, and change within a system. Periodical auditing of the logs can reveal unauthorized users and security flaws. Monitoring logs can help detect brute force attacks before they are successful.

External authentication

External authentication relies on a remote service to determine if users should have access to a system. External systems can offer flexibility for the system manager and convenience for the users. Users only have to log in once to access any information they need, and are authorized for, on the server.

Network and Client/Server Architectures

In the origin of the term **telecommunications,** it meant the transmission of computer data over the public telephone network. Today, the term refers to the broader scope of transmitting computer data over any network. What is a network? A **network** is a broader computer system that is created when two or more computers are linked together by **cables** and each computer needs to be equipped with a **network interface card** for plugging in the cables. Or the computers can be connected in a wireless network where each computer has a **wireless network adapter** that is equipped with an antenna.

All the computers are that are connected to the same network are said to be **on the network** and can be called a **network node**. When a node is active on the network it is **online** and when it is not active it is **offline**. A computer can be offline due to the request of the user or due to some type of computer or network malfunction. Networking is a way to share files of information, to share resources like printers, to use one master copy of a software program or to send messages. Once a computer is a network node, it is technically no longer a "personal" computer because some resources are shared with others.

LOCAL AREA NETWORK

A **local area network (LAN)** is a network of nodes that are in close physical proximity. Network nodes are generally tied together with network cables; however, with advances in technology, many LAN's are migrating towards wireless technology. In a wired network, a hardware device known as a **network hub** is needed as a central location for the wiring and all network nodes are connected to this central hub.

There are two main **LAN architectures**: peer-to-peer and client/server. In **peer-topeer** architecture, all the nodes have access to the public files on every other node; in effect, all nodes are equal peers. In **client/server** architecture, one central computer is called the server. The server holds the central files and software and the client pro-grams residing on the computers in the network access and modify the data that is on the server. This is the network architecture that is used by most business applications today. The main database is stored on the **server** computer and numerous workers access this data from network nodes. Picture an insurance company that has a customer service call center. Any customer service representative can answer a call and retrieve a policy holder's status from the server and update the information as required.

In a particular network there can be more than one computer that is designated as a server. It is best that each server is dedicated to a particular function. A **file server** is a computer on the client/server network that stores the application programs and data files that are used by the workstations in the network. In a peer-to-peer network, every workstation functions as a file server because all other network nodes can access the public files on every other network node. A file server is responsible for **locking** data to keep multiple network nodes from attempting to update the same data simultaneously.

A **print server** is a computer that is dedicated solely to managing the flow of output files to one or more printers. A print server is needed by companies that use expensive printers because they generate lots of documents and reports. While the same computer can be used as both a file server and a print server, it is usually recommended that these two functions be placed on separate computers when there are numerous network nodes.

For specialized large business applications, a file server might be coupled with a database server. While a file server holds all kinds of files and may contain database files, a **database server** contains only the major database files for the large application. A dedicated computer is needed to process the large database files efficiently.

Companies with a significant Internet presence will also dedicate a **web server** to their web site. Similarly, another server can be dedicated to e-mail messaging and it is called a **mail server**. The e-mail handling program on the workstations must be compatible with the e-mail handling software on the server.

The terminology for clients and servers becomes fuzzy because it applies to both hardware and database applications. In hardware terms, server can mean any computer that is dedicated as a file server, a print server, a database server, a web server or a mail server or in software terms it can mean any computer that has the main application program and database. However, the term client usually applies only to the software programs that reside on the workstations in the network, which may be called client workstations or client computers.

Be sure to read questions on the exam referring to client/server carefully and remember that the server is in charge, controlling all updates to the database it holds. Clients are the workstations or the computers that hold the client software; clients send requests for information or database updates (changes) to the server.

Along with two forms of architecture are three forms of network topology. The term **network topology** refers to the arrangement of nodes as either centralized or decentralized. In a centralized or **star network** all the nodes are connected to a central computer that controls all access to the network. While this form of LAN provides greater security and central management, a star network is expensive to install because each node requires a separate cable link to the hub. In a decentralized topology, nodes are connected together directly. In a **bus network,** the nodes are connected one to the next in a continuous fashion. This is very inexpensive but if any connection between two nodes fails, the entire network fails. The final traditional form of network topology is the decentralized **ring network** which is a bus network where the last node is connected to the first node, forming a loop. With the capability of two-way communication, any break in the connection no longer takes down the network.

Since computers in a network are no longer functioning as personal computers, a regular operating system like Windows that controls only directly connected peripherals is no longer adequate. Any personal computers that are in network require a network operating system.

A **network operating system (NOS)** has features for administering the network (keeping track of users and connections), back-up features for the server, security restrictions, and software for controlling the shared usage of peripheral devices. The NOS is also responsible for handling all communications between the computers in the network, which also may be called **workstations** in network terminology. Windows NT is an example of a network operating system. Windows Server, Novell Netware and Linux are examples of network operating systems for client/server networks.

After all this discussion, what are the necessary features of a network? The network requires two or more computers that are linked together with a network operating system that provides a **network protocol**, which is the method that the operating system uses to lock data.

There needs to be cabling or wireless connections between the network nodes and the operating system must provide a means of sharing the peripheral devices, which may also be called input and output media. Finally, every node in the network needs to have a unique identifier or **network address** that differentiates it from every other network node. While most networks in operation today use dedicated servers, a server is not required, especially for peer-to-peer networks.

The **network protocol** is a method for controlling a workstation's access to the public data on the network. For example, two users cannot be updating the same file at the same time. Why would two users want the same file? Much of software development is done by a team of programmers and several team members might need to work on the same document, each adding their own chapter, for example. If the network didn't enforce file locking, when it comes time to save the latest copy, one person's updates could be overwritten by someone else.

Carrier sense multiple access with collision detection (CSMA/CD) is one method for controlling access to public data. Using this method, each network node has an equal right to access the communication channel to the public data. If two nodes attempt to access the same data simultaneously, the network operating system decides which request to honor first by generating a random number. This method works quite well for small to medium size networks.

However, for large networks, other access methods are used. **Token passing** requires the implementation of a **token**, which is a particular pattern of bits; the token is passed like a baton in a relay race from workstation to workstation. Only the network node that currently has the "baton" or token is allowed to send or receive public data on the network. Like CSMA/CD, token passing gives equal opportunity to send and receive data to all network nodes.

WIDE AREA NETWORK

In contrast to a local area network (LAN) is a wide area network. A **wide area network (WAN)** links computers that are not in physical proximity. This terminology reflects the early history of networking prior to the development of the Internet. In the earlier days of networking, large companies with scattered locations would develop their own proprietary WAN to serve their own needs.

NETWORK CABLING

Before the advent of today's wireless technology, all networks required cables that physically attached the network nodes, also called workstations or just computers, together for a peer-to-peer network or to a central hub or network server in a client/server architecture. Many existing networks still use cabling, as do many new in-office networks. The cabling is not out-of-date just yet.

Several standards defines network cabling. You simply can't just plug one device into another and expect them to communicate. Remember that the operating system of the computers, both workstations, and servers, must be able to translate the signals to achieve proper communication between all nodes of the network as well as with the peripheral devices.

Historically, there are three standards for network cabling: ARCnet, Ethernet, and token ring. ARCnet is an older version of networking that was developed for the original IBM personal or mainframe computers and supported a star topology, a token-passing protocol, twisted pair or coaxial cable, and ARCnet network interface cards. A token ring network is a combination of a ring and star topology that uses a token-passing network protocol and twisted pair cable. IBM introduced This network form in 1986 and supported 255 workstations.

Today, most businesses use the Ethernet cabling standard, developed by Xerox Corporation. An Ethernet network can have up to 1,024 network nodes in a bus topology. Ethernet uses carrier sense multiple access with collision detection (CSMA/CD).

One of the latest forms of high-speed cabling for sophisticated networks is fiber-optic cable, which is constructed from thin fibers of glass rather than copper wire like twisted-pair cables. Laser light is transmitted, and at the receiving end, optical detectors transform the light into digital signals. Fiber-optic cable is currently both expensive and difficult to work with.

COMMUNICATIONS PROTOCOL

When information is passed between network nodes or transferred from one computer to another via telecommunications, a **communications protocol** or standard is required so that both computers understand the signals and treat them the same way. There are several communications protocols in use today:

- **Asynchronous** – the transmission of bits is not synchronized by a clock signal but is accomplished by sending the bits one after another, with a start and stop bit to mark the beginning and end of each data unit. Telephone lines can be used for this protocol.
- **Synchronous** – data is transmitted at very high speeds by using circuits that synchronize data transfer with electronic clock signals. Computers in high-speed mainframe networks use this protocol.
- **Full-duplex** – asynchronous transmission that allows the communications channel to send and receive signals at the same time.
- **Half-duplex** – also called local echo; asynchronous transmission that can handle only one signal at a time, alternating between the two computers.
- **Double-duplex** – full-duplex transmission with a sender and a receiver at each end that transmits simultaneously in both directions.
- **Echoplex** – the receiving computer acknowledges that it received the data by echoing the data back to the transmitting computer.
- **Parallel** – synchronous transmission through a parallel port to a peripheral device that is usually a parallel printer; the printer signals whether or not it is ready to receive additional data.

MODEM AND FAX

A **modem** is a peripheral device that allows signals to be sent from the computer to another computer over the telephone lines. The term modem stands for modulator/demodulator. Originally, a modem was an external device but today's personal computersare sold with a built-in modem. The modem has a fixed speed at which it is designed to transmit digital data that it converts to analog signals before transmission. **Analog signals** are sound-based signals that can be transmitted over the telephone lines. At the other end, the signals are converted from analog to digital once again.

A **fax machine** is an electronic device that transmits or receives an image of a printed page over the telephone line. A fax machine can also be connected as a shared peripheral device in a network or a fax capability can incorporated into a fax modem.

Operating Systems

The **operating system** is the base software of the computer that deals directly with the basic hardware components of the computer. There are five key functions of an operating system:

- System supervision – manage memory, control programs and processes
- Hardware services – controls devices like the hard drive and monitor
- Software services – provide file system support and user interfaces
- Communication services – controls communication with external systems or within the local network
- Security – controls access to the system and files

The memory manager is in charge of allocating RAM for a program to run in. Operating systems can support one of two types of memory management: monoprogramming, where only one program can run at a time, or multiprogramming, where one or more programs can reside in RAM and execute simultaneously. In multiprogramming, programs may not run exactly simultaneously but run concurrently with the operating system, allowing one program to run for a while and then switching to another.

There are several techniques that can be used to achieve multiprogramming in the operating system. One is partitioning, where several programs are moved into a fixed area of RAM called a partition. In this scheme, the operating system alternates between the programs as already described. The other is paging. A program is divided into page segments; the advantage of paging is that the smaller page segments can be loaded into any available page in RAM. Think of pages as a large number of small partitions. Paging is flexible. Partitioning requires a lot of contiguous memory, while paging allows the pages to be scattered. Paging is a form of virtual memory where parts of a program are stored on the hard disk. The term thrashing describes the unusual condition of a program that requires the operating system to swap virtual memory pages inefficiently.

The process manager, a key player in the operating system, manages programs that are currently executing in memory, which are referred to as processes in many operating system environments. A process typically executes in memory until it needs some input or output (I/O) function, for example, waiting for user input from the keyboard or writing data to the hard disk. Or it executes until it uses up the CPU time allocated to it by the operating system or until the process completes. Understanding the process manager's role is crucial in comprehending the functioning of an operating system.

In the meantime, the device manager manages the access to the I/O devices. Another name for the device manager is the I/O supervisor. I/O devices are significantly slower than the CPU's speed, so the process must wait until the I/O operation is complete before continuing to execute. The device manager monitors the device to ensure that it is turned on and ready to process; it maintains a list or queue of processes that need to access the device; and it determines which processes access the device based upon priorities set in the operating system. Each device, such as a printer, needs a device driver, a program that provides the operating system with the information it needs to work with the device.

A spooler is a program within the operating system that sends requests for printing on a printer to a file on disk rather than directly to the printer. The device manager thinks that it is printing to a high-speed printer, but all the printed output is being collected on the hard disk and printed as continuous pages at a later time. Otherwise, processes would be stalled as they waited while one process "hogged" the printer.

Some CPU's and their operating systems utilize the concept of an interrupt, a signal to the CPU that a process needs to stop momentarily to process an I/O or some other type of request, including error interrupts. The interrupt handler, a program within the operating system, plays a critical role in analyzing the interrupt signal to determine its type. If the signal is an I/O request, the interrupt handler passes the request to the device manager or I/O supervisor. Understanding the interrupt handler's function is essential in understanding how an operating system manages I/O requests.

There are several properties of operating systems that apply to how requested programs execute, and it is important to understand the different terms because they are easily confused:

- **Batch processing** – typical of mainframe computers with a large number of users; a program or series of programs are executed under the control of the operating system without interaction with a user. The user "submits" a batch request and the operating system schedules the execution based on priorities set

by management and the user is informed when the task is complete. In a PC operating system, batch files have the suffix .BAT. Batch processing is suitable for tasks that are routine and periodic in nature that can wait until computer resources are available. Batch processing is efficient because all transactions of the same type are processed together.
- **Real-time** – immediate processing of transactions as they occur. Real-time systems are the same as online processing and require online random or direct access files.
- **Multiple program loading** – an operating system that lets the user start more than one program at a time; however, only one of the programs is active at a time.
- **Multiprocessing** – the simultaneous execution of different portions of a program by a multiprocessor, a computer with more than one CPU. This type of processing requires an operating system that is capable of parallel processing.
- **Multitasking** – the execution of more than one program at a time on a computer system; one task executes in the foreground and interfaces with the user. Another program that does not require interface with a user executes in the background. An example of a background task is printing spooled output while the user is on the Internet.
- **Multiprogramming** – same as multiple program loading.
- **Multithreading** – a form of multitasking where multiple tasks run under the same program. For example, one copy of a word processor might be being used by several workstations at the same time.
- **Fault tolerant computing** – the ability of the system to produce correct results and continue processing even if hardware or software errors have occurred. This can be accomplished by redundant computer components that duplicate processing or error correcting memory.

The term **boot** is used to refer to the process required to clear RAM memory, load the operating system and prepare the computer for use. This term comes from the earliest days of computing. A **cold boot** occurs whenever the computer is powered on and a **warm boot** occurs when the user requests a system restart. An equivalent term for boot is **reboot.**

In addition to the operating system are **system support programs** that provide common useful functions, for example, produce a screen image or printout of the files on a hard disk. Such programs are called **system utilities**. As a group, these programs are known as **system software**.

 Software Development Methods and Tools

METHODS

One software development method is the traditional software or **systems development** which is an 8-step process required to construct an information system that addressesa particular problem, such as implementing an online reservation system. Synonymous terms are **information system development, application development,** or **waterfall model**.

A properly implemented information system development progresses through eight well-defined stages:

- **Systems investigation** – the feasibility stage where a go/no go evaluation is performed to determine if it is cost-effective to implement the system.
- **Feasibility studies** (or preliminary studies) – preliminary studies that investigate the needs of prospective users, resource needs, costs and benefits of the new system are done during this stage.
- **Systems analysis** – the tasks are to define the business problem, gather information about the existing approach or system, and determine the **functional requirements** for the new system. The analysis stage defines *what* the system will do.
- **Systems design** – the tasks are to define *how* the system will accomplish the requirements. The output of this phase is a **system specification** that includes the definition of:
  - System inputs, outputs and user interfaces.
  - Any hardware, software, networking, procedures and staff needed to implement the system.
  - How the components are integrated and how transactions flow through the system.
- **Programming** – translating the design into computer code using a programming language.
- **Testing** – testing the code to ascertain that it will produce the desired results for every case.
- **Implementation** – conversion of the old system to the new system.
- **Operation** – the new system is placed into use.
- **Maintenance** – after the system is placed into operation, previously undetected errors must be corrected, updates made to handle changing requirements, and minor improvements or upgrades added.

Another application method is prototyping. **Prototyping** focuses on end-user requirements without doing feasibility studies or writing a specification. Prototyping is most suitable for smaller applications or for developing the user-interface portion of a large application.

Rapid application development (RAD) employs **CASE (Computer-Assisted Software Engineering) tools** to automate many of the tasks in the traditional systems-development model. CASE tools include diagramming tools, analysis tools, document storage tools, documentation generators, and code generators.

Object-oriented development also differs from the traditional systems development model in that the approach emphasizes the use of "objects" which are aspects of the real world that must be modeled by the application system rather than the step-by-step processing that is needed. An object-oriented approach to a billing application should be amenable to other mailings as well because the real-world functions are similar.

TOOLS

There are two traditional tools for managing the systems development. A **Gantt chart** shows the amount of time allocated for each step in the systems development process. Of course, in business, each of the eight steps is broken down into hundreds of finer-grained tasks so there are many Gantt charts used to allocate and track time.

PERT (Program Evaluation and Review Techniques) charts are a powerful tool for project managers to plan, schedule, and coordinate tasks within a project. These charts provide a visual representation of the interrelationship between tasks, emphasizing the project's dependencies and critical path. By clearly illustrating which tasks must be completed before others can begin, PERT charts help project managers optimize resource allocation, identify potential bottlenecks, and ensure that the project stays on track.

The main feature of a PERT chart is its ability to show the connections between tasks as network nodes. Each node represents a specific task, and the arrows connecting the nodes indicate the dependencies between them. For example, if Task B cannot start until Task A is complete, an arrow will be drawn from Node A to Node B. This visual representation allows project managers to quickly grasp the sequence of tasks and the overall flow of the project.

One of the key benefits of using a PERT chart is its ability to highlight the critical path of the project. The critical path is the longest sequence of dependent tasks determining the minimum time required to complete the project. By identifying the critical path, project managers can focus their attention on the tasks that have the greatest impact on the project's timeline and allocate resources accordingly.

For instance, consider a software development project that involves designing, coding, testing, and deploying a new application. A PERT chart for this project might show that the design phase (Task A) must be completed before coding (Task B) can begin, and coding must be finished before testing (Task C) can start. If the design phase takes longer than expected, it will delay the start of coding and, consequently, the entire project. By recognizing this dependency, the project manager can prioritize the design phase and ensure it is completed on time to avoid delays in subsequent tasks.

Another example of how PERT charts can be useful is in the construction industry. Building a house involves numerous tasks, such as laying the foundation, framing, electrical work, plumbing, and roofing. A PERT chart can help the construction manager visualize the dependencies between these tasks and plan accordingly. For instance, the chart would show that the foundation (Task A) must be laid before framing (Task B) can begin, and electrical work (Task C) and plumbing (Task D) must be completed before drywall installation (Task E) can start. By understanding these relationships, the construction manager can efficiently schedule subcontractors and materials deliveries, minimizing delays and ensuring a smooth workflow.

PERT charts also facilitate communication among team members and stakeholders. By providing a clear, visual representation of the project's tasks and dependencies, PERT charts help everyone involved understand their roles and responsibilities, as well as how their work fits into the overall project timeline. This transparency can foster collaboration, accountability, and a shared sense of purpose among team members.

PERT charts are an invaluable tool for project managers across various industries. By visually representing the interrelationship of tasks and highlighting dependencies, these charts enable managers to optimize project schedules, allocate resources effectively, and identify potential issues before they cause significant delays. Using specific examples, such as software development and construction projects, it becomes clear how PERT charts can be applied to improve project planning, communication, and overall success.

A **system flowchart** may be used during the systems design stage to illustrate in diagram form how the system is constructed in terms of files, processing, inputs and outputs. A commonly used set of symbols is employed when constructing any type of flowchart. The system flowchart typically emphasizes the physical devices that are used by the system. Detail level flowcharts that emphasize the logical structure of processing may also be constructed for every process in the system before programming begins. Similarly, a **data flow diagram** can show the logical relationship of data to the external entities like departments within the business.

PSEUDOCODE

After the system specification is complete but before the design is coded in the actual programming language, portions of the system may be coded in what is called **pseudocode,** a design technique that lays out the processing in a simple but standardized language so that the logic can be examined before it is translated into the more complex programming language.

Before delving into pseudocode we must consider how expressions are processed in most computers. Expression processing uses concepts from algebra for computing the results of evaluating expressions. In most computer languages as well as in pseudocode the normal symbols + for add, for subtract, * for multiply, and / for divide are used.

Exponentiation, or raising a number to a power, has various representations in the different languages and for our discussion here we will use the symbol ** which is used in several languages and in pseudocode.

The expression A + B * C means to take the value of A, B, and C and perform the indicated operations. However, the rules of **operator precedence** apply when there are no parentheses in the expression. In the absence of parentheses the rule of operator precedence from highest precedence to lowest precedence is:

1) any exponentiation is evaluated first
2) followed by any multiplication or division in their order of appearance from left to right
3) followed by any addition or subtraction in their order of appearance

So for our simple example, if A has the value 2, B is 3, and C is 4, the expression value is 3 * 4 + 2 which is 14.

However, if parentheses are added to the expression, expressions in parentheses are evaluated first, starting with innermost parentheses. Within parentheses, the above operator precedence rule still applies. If we rewrite our simple expression to

(A + B) * C we now add A and B to get 5; then multiply by 4 to get 20.

Continuing to use the same values, A is 2, B is 3, and C is 4:

1) C – A ** 2 is 0
2) A + B * C ** 2 is 82
3) (A + B) * C ** 2 is 80
4) ((A + B) * C) ** 2 is 400

Pseudocode resembles English and contains the following simple statements which are sufficient to describe any process:

- **Sequence** – an ordered series of simple actions like computations. The pseudocode code statement is SET.
- **Decision branching** – tests a relationship in the process (called a **condition**) and performs one sequence if the relationship is true and a different sequence if the relationship is false. The pseudocode statement is

    IF (condition) … THEN…ELSE…END IF.
- **Repetition** – continue to perform a sequence of actions while a condition is true. Skip to the sequence following the repetition when the condition becomes false. The pseudocode statement is WHILE (condition)…END WHILE.

A condition can be a comparison. Possible comparisons are:
= tests if the two values are the same;
> tests if the left operand is greater than the right operand;
< tests if the left operand is smaller than the right operand;
>= tests if the left operand is greater than or equal to the right operand;
<= tests if the left operand is less than or equal to the right operand.

A condition can use **logical operators**. The logical operators are AND, OR and NOT.
AND is true if both of the operators are true and false otherwise
OR is true if either or both of the operators are true and false otherwise
NOT reverses the value of true to false and false to true

Again continuing to use the same values, A is 2, B is 3, and C is 4:
A = B is false
A > B is false
A < B is true

The SET statement gives a value to a variable. An example of a sequence of pseudocode instructions using only SET instructions:

    SET A TO 2
gives A the value of 2
    SET B TO 3
    SET C TO 4
    SET C TO A + B
changes C from 4 to 5
    SET A TO B * C

changes A from 2 to 15. Why? The previous SET statement changed the value of C. The statements are an example of a sequence of actions that, if they were written in a programming language, the computer would execute in order.

The IF…THEN…ELSE…END IF statement is a decision branching statement that tests the condition specified in the IF clause. If the condition is true, the sequence of statements in the THEN clause is executed and the sequence of statements in the ELSE clause is skipped. If the condition is false, the sequence of instructions in the THEN clause is skipped and the sequence of statements in the ELSE clause is executed. In either case, after the THEN or ELSE sequence, execution goes to the statement after the END IF. Using the values of A, B, and C from the last example,

```
IF (A > B) THEN
    SET LARGER TO A
ELSE
    SET LARGER TO B
END IF
SET A TO 0
SET B TO 0
```

After this pseudocode is evaluated, what are the values of A, B, and LARGER? A started out as 15 and B was 3. Since 15 > 3 is true LARGER becomes 15, the ELSE clause is skipped and both A and B are set to zero. Which clause would be executed if A and B were equal? The condition (A > B) would be false so the ELSE clause is the one that would be executed.

Repetition is coded as a WHILE loop in pseudocode. The following example showing a **WHILE loop** in pseudocode instructions is from the CLEP sample test.

```
SET A TO 1
SET B TO 3
SET A TO A + B
WHILE A < 20
    SET A TO (A * A)/2
END WHILE
```

An important point about using a WHILE loop is that some statement within the WHILE and END WHILE pair must change a value in the condition that is being tested to eventually make the condition false otherwise the loop will run forever. In the above pseudocode A has the value of 4 when the sequence of instructions reaches the WHILE statement for the first time. Since 4 is less than 20, the condition is true and the sequence of statements within the WHILE loop is executed. The value of A changes to 4 * 4 / 2 which is 8. The sequence encounters the END WHILE and repetition causes the execution to return to the WHILE statement. The value of A is still less than 20 so the WHILE sequence is entered once again. This time A is set to 8 * 8 / 2 which is 32. The END WHILE is processed and repetition causes the WHILE to be evaluated again. This time A is greater than 20 and the processing skips to the non-existent sequence after the END WHILE. For this example, the final value of A is 32.

Note that A, B, and C are just arbitrary names for the values. The name given to a value can be any letter or descriptive name like:

SET AREA TO LENGTH * WIDTH

CONVERSION TO A NEW SYSTEM

Most information systems today are replacing an older or out-of-date existing system. There are four methods for converting use of the old system to the new system. **Parallel conversion** means that both the old and the new system are used simultaneously and the results are compared periodically to detect errors. **Phased conversion** puts only a portion of the new system into use at one time or allows only certain departments to begin using the system. **Pilot conversion** means that only one department or physical location is the first to use and test the new system. **Plunge** is the term given to the abrupt changeover to a new system without using one of the other conversion techniques first.

Programming Languages

At the outset, the only programming language available was **machine language**, which was unique to each model of computer and was programmed in binary using only 0's and 1's. Machine language was quickly replaced by **symbolic language** that replaced the binary number for an instruction with a defined acronym. The first symbolic languages were **assembly languages** because the acronyms were "assembled" into strings of 0's and 1's. Assembly language is still in active use today for special purpose computer applications.

Using assembly language requires that every CPU instruction must be coded by the programmer; therefore there is a one-to-one correspondence between a line of code in assembly language and a line of code in machine language. Assembly language has been superseded by **high level languages** that are independent of the instruction set of the CPU, resulting in code that can be executed on more than one model of CPU. High level languages are also an attempt to come closer to **natural language**, like English, when programming a computer.

With a high level language, the program must still be translated eventually into machine language for execution. After a program is written in a high level language, it is processed by another program called a **compiler** which performs the necessary translation into machine language.

WHAT IS THE DIFFERENCE BETWEEN A COMPILER AND AN INTERPRETER?

Computers do exactly what they are told to. The problem is that there are many different computer programming languages and different programs require different languages. Compilers are used to transform something written in one computer programming language, called the source language, into a machine language (such as binary code). Machine language is called the target language, so that it can be executed by the computer. Interpreters directly execute instructions written in a high level computer programming language. This is done by translating it into a language which the interpreter is able to execute instructions from. This is the main difference between the two. Compilers translate to machine language that the computer understands, and the interpreter translates to languages which it understands. Of the two, compilers are more common.

CATEGORIES OF HIGH LEVEL LANGUAGES

Today there are five categories of high level languages. The categories are listed below with examples of each type.

- **Procedural** – a set of instructions that are executed in the order indicated
    - **FORTRAN** (FORmula TRANslation) – early language available in 1957; ideal for scientific and engineering applications even today.
    - **BASIC** (Beginner's All-Purpose Symbolic Instruction Code) – developed in 1964 for teaching purposes; resurrected in the 1990's for use on personal computers because BASIC does not require a compiler.
    - **COBOL** (COmmon Business-Oriented Language) – available in the early 1960's for business applications; still in active use today. **Pascal** – available in the 1970's as a language for teaching students.
    - **C language** – also available in the early 1970's and developed for writing the UNIX operating system. Gained popularity as a general purpose language for implementing other kinds of systems.

- **Object-oriented** – programmer defines objects and the operations for each object
    - **C++** – has three main principles: 1) **encapsulation** or hiding the data inside the object; 2) **inheritance** whereby an object can inherit properties from another object; and 3) **polymorphism** that allows the programmer to define

multiple operations with the same name that do different processing in different classes. C++ is a general-purpose language based upon C.
- **Java** – based upon both C and C++. A program in Java can be either an application or an **applet,** a mini-program that is embedded in a Web document and executed by a browser after downloading. A **servlet** is an applet that runs on a server. Note: **JavaScript** was developed by Netscape to allow Java-like programming but it is not related to the Java language.

- **Functional** – defines a set of primitive functions and allows the programmer to combine these to create new functions. Functional languages are not used to implement information systems.
  - **Lisp** – defined in the early 1960's.

- **Declarative** – based on formal logic. Declarative languages are not used to implement information systems.
  - **Prolog** – defined in the early 1970's.

- **Special** – new languages that do not fit in the four traditional categories.
  - **HTML** (HyperText Markup Language) – is not a real programming language but it allows formatting instructions to be embedded in a file. The user's web browser interprets the formatting instructions when the file is displayed on the user's monitor. The file is composed of the text and formatting **tags** that are enclosed in angle brackets (< >). An HTML name and its parameters occur within the brackets. An HTML program is composed of a head and a body. The head contains the title and other browser parameters. The body contains the text and the formatting tags.
  - **PERL** (Practical Extraction and Report Language) – similar to C but adds the capability to scan text files, extract information from the text, and prepare a report from the information. PERL is in active use to create Common Gateway Interface (CGI) scripts that handle the output of HTML forms. PERL may also be called a **scripting language** as is JavaScript because they are used to produce a **script** or series of instructions that tells a program how to perform a specific procedure.
  - **SQL** (Structured Query Language) – a language that is used to interrogate a database.

| Samples for Common Programming Languages ||
Language	Code Sample
FORTRAN	WRITE (6,7) 7 FORMAT(13H Hello World!) STOP END

COBOL	IDENTIFICATION DIVISION.
	    PROGRAM-ID. HELLOWORLD.
	    PROCEDURE DIVISION.
	        PARA-1.
	        DISPLAY "Hello World!".
	        STOP RUN.	

BASIC	10 PRINT "Hello World!";	

Samples for Common Programming Languages	
C	```#include <stdio.h>

int main(void)
{
   printf("Hello World!\n");

   return 0;
}``` |
| Pascal | ```program HelloWorld(output);
begin
  writeln('Hello World!')
end.``` |
| C++ | ```#include <iostream>
#include <ostream>

int main()
{
  std::cout << "Hello World!" << std::endl;
  return 0;
}``` |
| C# | ```class HelloWorldClass
{
   static void Main()
   {
      System.Console.WriteLine("Hello, world!");
   }
}``` |

Visual FoxPro	loForm = CREATEOBJECT("HelloWorld") loForm.Show(1)
	
	DEFINE CLASS HiForm AS Form
	  AutoCenter = .T.
	  Caption = "Hello World!"
	
	  ADD OBJECT lblHi as Label WITH ;
	    Caption = "Hello World!"
	ENDDEFINE

Samples for Common Programming Languages	

Java	// HelloWorld.java
	public class HelloWorld {
	    public static void main(String[] args) {
	        System.out.println("Hello World!");
	    }
	}

HTML	Hello World!
HTML (output in italics)	\<i>Hello World!\</i>
HTML (output in bold)	\Hello World!\

User Interfaces

Today's interactive software relies heavily on the **graphical user interface (GUI)** which uses symbols to represent program or computer functions. These symbols are called **icons**. The GUI became popular after a team of researchers at Xerox Corporations found that people recognize graphic representations faster than they can read words or phrases. GUI's typically are comprised of pull-down menus, dialog boxes, check boxes, radio buttons, drop-down list boxes, scrollbars, navigational bars and the like. Programs that use GUI require more powerful computers with a sophisticated display monitor.

User interfaces must take into account the human being who is the intended user of the information system. **Ergonomics**, the science of designing machines, computers, and physical work areas so that people find them easy to use, is an important consideration in the design of GUI's. Making a start button pink and a stop button yellow goes against lifelong training that green means go and red means stop and is not an ergonomically sound design choice.

Presentation graphics are designed to present information in graphical form, like line or bar graphs or pie charts, that helps illustrate trends and relationships in the data in order to help managers and users make better informed decisions. This type of information is easier to grasp in a visual rather than numeric format.

Multimedia presentations integrate multiple media like text, graphics, voice and other sound, photographs and video clips and are gaining in popularity as well. **Hypermedia** is the term given to a hypertext system that uses multimedia resources where **hypertext** is a method of preparing and publishing text so that the user can select their own path through the material. **Hyperlinks**, which are underlined words or phrases, display another page of information when the user clicks on the link with a mouse. This type of user interface leaves users in complete control of how they navigate the information rather than being forced to view the information sequentially in the order established by someone else.

Interactive video systems combine image processing with text, audio and video capabilities. Software exists for producing these **digital video interactive (DVI)** applications.

Software Packages

Software applications can be divided into two classes:

- **Proprietary** – an information processing application that was developed by staff in a particular company or contracted with a software development company for use solely by the company.
- **Off-the-shelf or package** – software designed for general use that can be purchased or leased from a software vendor.

There are numerous familiar types of software packages such as:

- **Data management software** – supports potentially massive database files.
- **Word processing** – supports production of documents.
- **Desktop publishing** – incorporates photographs, diagrams, and other images with text to produce sophisticated documents equivalent to those produced at a printing house.
- **Graphics software** – allows the user to convert data to a graphical form.

- **Presentation graphics software** – typically contains drawing tools and other presentation aids for creating professional-looking audience presentations.
- **Analysis graphics** – graphically represents data that has been analyzed statistically.
- **CAD (Computer-Aided Design) Software** – supports advanced engineering design.
- **Multimedia software** – handles multiple media for input or output of data, particularly the combination of spatial-based media like text and images with time-based media like sound and video.
- **Interactive multimedia software** – allows the user to control the flow of information; used in museums and information kiosks.
- **Communications software** – supports interconnection of computers. Network operating systems are an example of a sophisticated communications software package.
- **Speech recognition software** – software that provides for recognition of human speech in real-time.
- **Decision support system (DSS)** – software that aids in management decision making.
- **Groupware** – software that promotes communication and collaboration among a group of people who are typically co-workers.
- **Software suite** – a collection of related software packages from the same vendor that are bundled together at one price.

Data Management

DATA CONCEPTS AND DATA STRUCTURES

The simple pseudocode language that was introduced earlier relied solely on the concept of a simple **variable**, a single location in memory that can store just one value. From the almost absurd examples of pseudocode, it is easy to see that programming with just variables is not particularly useful. The power of information systems lies in their ability to process vast quantities of similar information, like all customers, all inventory or all suppliers.

A **data structure** defines a collection of related variables that can be processed either individually or as a whole. Procedural programming languages support some advanced data structures but the latest database management systems are needed for handling much of the real-time processing that occurs today.

Procedural languages like FORTAN and COBOL use a data structure called an array for storing items in a list. Think of an array like a grocery shopping list where every item on the list can be found in one grocery store. An **array** is a fixed-size sequenced collection of elements all having the same data type. A **data type** defines what kind of values can be stored in a variable or other data structure element, such as integer or text. A **subscript** is used to select which element of the array to process, where the subscript is usually a simple variable like the A, B or C in the examples that is incremented by one as it steps through the elements of the array. The grocery list is an example of a **onedimensional array** and a table with rows and columns is a **two-dimensional array.** Arrays are always stored in the computer's memory when the program is running.

A **record** is a collection of related elements, usually with different data types. A record is given a record name and each element in the record is called a **field**. An example of a record is customer data with a name, address, and dollar amount owed. Records are stored in files on the hard disk and must be read and rewritten in order to be processed.

Procedural languages can process two types of files: sequential and random. A **sequential file** must be read from disk from beginning to end. In order to process any record, the entire file needs to be accessed. Sequential files are useful when all of the data items must be processed on a routine basis. In a **random file** any record can be accessed as long as the **record key**, for example the customer account number, is known. Historically, sequential and random files were used primarily in batch processing mainframe systems. A random file can also be called a **direct access file**.

DATABASE MANAGEMENT SYSTEMS

A database management system goes beyond the capabilities of the original file systems and allows the definition, creation, and maintenance of a database. A **database** is a collection of related information about a particular subject organized in such a way as to facilitate retrieval and update. A **database management system (DBMS)** is a set of computer programs that controls the creation, maintenance and use of the databases of an organization. A DBMS facilitates the organization of data by providing sorting and grouping options for reports. The **data dictionary** is a database of all the names and descriptions of all types of data records and their interrelationships.

A database management system is designed based upon one of several **database data models**: hierarchical, network, relational, distributed, object-oriented or hypermedia. In the **hierarchical model,** which is obsolete in today's technology, data is stored as an upside down tree-structure with a root at the highest level and data stored down the branches. It is an example of a **one-to-many** relationship among the records because one root has many branches.

The **network model** can represent more complicated data with **many-to-many** relationships. The data is organized like a hierarchy but information at any level can point to multiple pieces of information at a subordinate level. Network models are also obsolete.

Today the database management systems are based upon the **relational model** which makes the data appear as a **relation,** a two-dimensional table. Note that this is not how the data is actually stored on the hard disk. Every relation in the database has a name and one or more attributes, where the attributes define the columns of the table. Each column of the table defines a distinct data element.

The **distributed model** is simply a relational model where the data is distributed over one or more computers that may or may not be in the same physical location. The **object-oriented model** is related to object-oriented programming and consists of objects, attributes, classes, methods and messages. In a **hypermedia or hypertext model** the relationships between data elements is less structured than in a traditional database because the elements define text, graphics, sound or full-motion video.

A database management system provides support for organizing the data and retrieving it in sorted or grouped order for reporting purposes. **Structured query language (SQL)** is the means used to interrogate the database and retrieve groups of records for analysis. A **data warehouse** is a relational database management system that is designed to support management decision making. Data is usually stored differently in the warehouse than in the operational database. A **data mart** is a smaller version of a data warehouse that focuses on one subject area. **Data mining** provides a mechanism for extracting previously unknown trends or forecasts from the data in a data warehouse or data mart.

There are many advantages to using a database management system. The DBMS, especially through use of the data dictionary, promotes the standardization of data. The DBMS consolidates the data so that it does not need to be duplicated and stored in many files across the organization. Rather than needing many different programs to process the data, all data access is done through the DBMS. Data is accessible and shared among all users and a common security system to protect data is in place.

HYPERTEXT AND HYPERMEDIA

Hypertext and hypermedia are revolutionary concepts transforming how we interact with and consume information in the digital age. Hypertext is a methodology that allows for the interactive reading of documents stored in a text database. It enables users to navigate the document by clicking on hyperlinks, embedded references that connect related pieces of information. This non-linear approach to reading allows users to explore the document in a way that suits their interests and needs rather than following a predetermined sequence.

Hypertext documents typically contain text and a limited number of graphics, such as images and diagrams. The hyperlinks within the document can lead to other sections of the same document or to external sources, providing a seamless and interconnected reading experience. Software packages like Adobe Acrobat and Microsoft Word have built-in features for creating hypertext documents, making it easier for authors to incorporate hyperlinks and create interactive content.

Hypermedia, on the other hand, takes the concept of hypertext a step further by incorporating multiple forms of media, including text, graphics, audio, and video. This allows for a more immersive and engaging experience, as users can interact with various types of content within a single document. For example, a hypermedia document about a historical event might include text descriptions, images of relevant artifacts, audio recordings of eyewitness accounts, and video clips of reenactments or documentaries.

The combination of hypertext and hypermedia has given rise to electronic books or e-books. E-books are digital versions of traditional printed books that can be read on electronic devices such as smartphones, tablets, and dedicated e-readers like Amazon Kindle or Kobo. They offer several advantages over physical books, including portability, searchability, and the ability to include interactive elements like hyperlinks and multimedia content.

One notable example of a hypermedia e-book is "Our Choice" by Al Gore, which explores the topic of climate change. The e-book features interactive graphics, animations, and documentary videos that enhance the reading experience and provide a deeper understanding of the subject matter. Another example is "The Wasteland" by T.S. Eliot, which has been adapted into a hypermedia edition that includes audio recordings of the poem, annotations, and scholarly commentary.

The educational sector has also embraced hypertext and hypermedia, with many textbooks and learning materials now available in digital formats. For instance, "Principles of Biology" by Nature Education is an interactive online textbook incorporating hyperlinks, animations, and quizzes to engage students and reinforce key concepts.

As technology continues to advance, the possibilities for hypertext and hypermedia are expanding. With the increasing availability of virtual and augmented reality devices, we can expect to see even more immersive and interactive forms of electronic books in the future. The integration of hypertext and hypermedia has revolutionized how we consume and interact with information, providing a more dynamic and personalized reading experience.

DOCUMENT IMAGES

Image processing has revolutionized the way we handle documents. It enables the electronic capture, storage, processing, and retrieval of document images containing various types of content, such as numeric data, typed text, handwriting, graphics, and photographs. This technology has found widespread applications in industries ranging from healthcare and finance to legal services and government institutions.

One example of image processing in action is the digitization of medical records. Healthcare providers can scan patient files, including handwritten notes, test results, and X-ray images, and store them electronically. This allows for quick and easy access to patient information, streamlining the healthcare process and improving patient care.

Similarly, financial institutions use image processing to digitize and process checks, loan applications, and other financial documents. By automating these processes, banks can reduce errors, improve efficiency, and provide faster customer service.

Electronic Document Management (EDM) systems take image processing further by integrating additional features and functionalities. These systems not only handle document images but can also incorporate voice messages, word processors, and desktop publishing tools. For instance, a law firm might use an EDM system to manage case files, including scanned legal documents, recorded depositions, and electronically drafted contracts.

Another example of an EDM system is a content management system (CMS) used by a publishing company. The CMS allows authors to submit their work electronically, editors to collaborate on revisions, and designers to create layouts using desktop publishing tools. The final product, such as a magazine or book, can be stored and distributed electronically.

The integration of image processing and EDM systems has greatly enhanced our ability to manage and access information, making document-intensive processes more efficient and cost-effective. As technology advances, we can expect to see even more sophisticated applications of these tools in various industries.

Data Models

Data models graphically represent the composition of and relationship between data in a database system. Three common types of data models are the entity-relationship (E-R) model, semantic object model and relational model.

Entity-Relationship Model

E-R models, developed by Peter Chen in 1976, look at four elements: entities, relationships, attributes, and identifiers.

Entities

In E-R models, an **entity** is something that can be identified and tracked within the system environment. For a retail store, an entity may be a piece of merchandise, an employee, an order or a cash register. All similar entities can be considered as a single unity – an **entity class**. A particular entity within an entity class is called an **instance**. For example, all of the accounts in a bank can be grouped together as an entity class. Account number 1234 is an instance within that class.

Relationships

The association between two or more entities is called a **relationship**. If the relation is between entire entity classes, it is called a **relationship class**. If it is only between certain instances, it is called a relationship instance. The **degree** of a relationship is the number of entities involved. **Binary relationships** are common in systems. Binary relationships occur between two entities. In other words, they are of degree 2. The following chart describes the degrees of some sample relationships.

DEGREES OF SAMPLE RELATIONSHIPS		
Relationship Description	*Entities Involved*	*Degree*
A company hires an architect and a contractor to construct a building	Client Architect Contractor	3
One person owns several residences	Person Residence	2
One teacher teachers several classes	Teacher Classes	2
Each student in a class is assigned a study partner	Students	1

Attributes

An entity's characteristics are called its **attributes**. Consider a piece of merchandise in a retail store. It may have some of the following attributes: size, price, color, and manufacturer. Like entities, relationships can have attributes.

Identifiers

Certain incidences within entity groups may share many attributes. For instance, there may be many shirts in a store that are the same color. In order to be tracked, an individual incidence needs an attribute that is unique. The attribute that describes a particular incidence and no other is called the **identifier**. Serial numbers, social security numbers and account numbers are common identifiers in information systems. Some systems may require more than one attribute to uniquely identify an incidence. These identifiers are called **composite identifiers**.

Creating E-R Diagrams

E-R diagrams may take a variety of forms. The standard is to use rectangles to show entity classes and diamonds to show relationships.

Binary relationships are the most common type of relationship in information systems. They can be divided into three types. If a single instance of an entity class is related to a single instance of another class, the relationship is called **1:1** ("one to one"). If one instance of an entity class can be related to many instances of another class, the relationship is called **1:N** ("one to many" or "one to N"). If many instances of each class can be involved in the relationship, the relationship is called **N:M** ("many to many" or "N to M").

The maximum cardinality of the relationship is labeled inside the diamond. The **maximum cardinality** is the maximum number of entity instances that can be involved on each side of the relationship.

The following table shows the type and maximum cardinality of some binary relationships.

EXAMPLE RELATIONSHIPS		
Relationship Description	*Type of Binary Relationship*	*Maximum Cardinality*
Each apartment in a building has a phone line.	1:1	1:1
A high school student can take up to six classes a semester.	1:N	1:6
A person can belong to several civic organizations, and each organization can have several members.	N:M	N:M

In an E-R diagram, ellipses represent attributes. The ellipses are connected to the entities they describe by lines.

The following E-R diagrams illustrates the relationship between apartments and telephone lines.

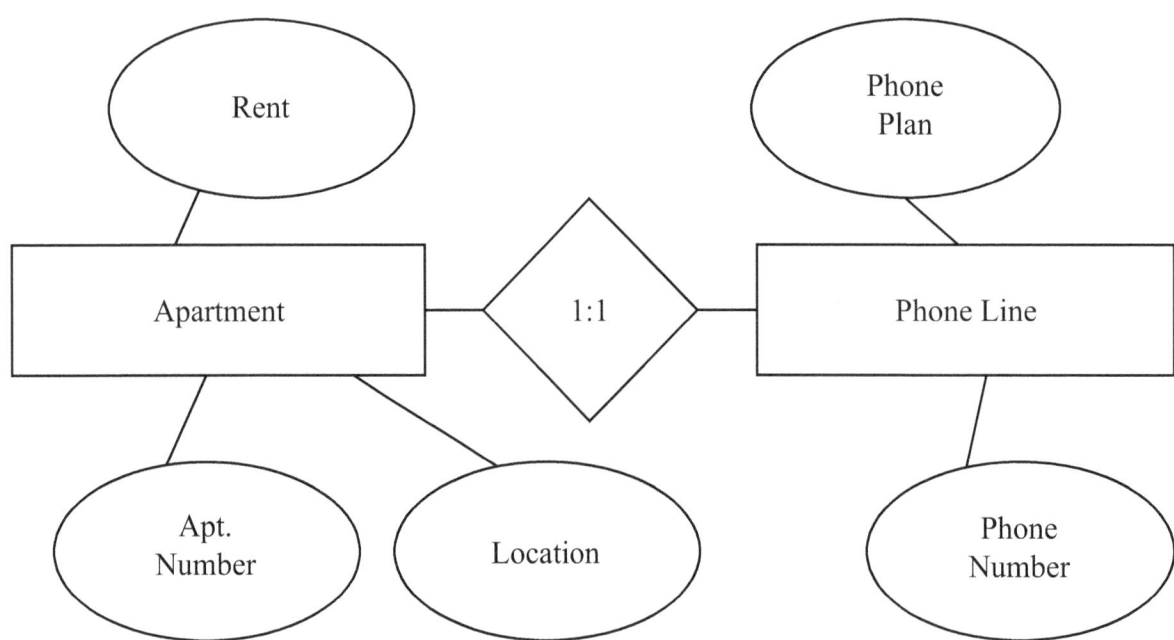

Semantic Object Model

Systems can be thought of as a collection of semantic, or meaningful, objects. Like entities in the E-R model, semantic objects represent identifiable things, have attributes, and can be grouped into classes. Unlike entities, semantic objects can have attributes that describe their relationship to other objects. For example, the semantic object EMPLOYEE may have attributes such as "name," "Social security number," and "position." It may also have the object attribute "department," which links the object to another semantic object, DEPARTMENT. DEPARTMENT may include attributes such as "address," "office number" and "fax number" that describe the department where the employee works.

Relational Model

The relational model is a more general way of representing information systems, especially databases.

Relational models are based on relations – two-dimensional tables of data. The rows of a relation are called **tuples** and the columns are called **attributes**. Each cell of the relation must be a single value, and all cells in an attribute must be of the same kind (for example, telephone number, name or transaction number). Each attribute must have a unique name. Each tuple must be unique, and the order of the tuples and attributes must be insignificant.

Any table that is a relation is not necessarily an efficient database design. **Normalization** is a process of breaking down relations to make better structures. Normalization optimizes database performance by reducing data redundancy.

 Hierarchy of Data

When referring to data, a hierarchy (or "tree") is a structure where the only relationships are one-to-many. Each element in a hierarchy is called a node. The relationships between the nodes are called branches. The element immediately above a node is called its parent. The nodes immediately below and related to a node are called its children. The root of the tree is the top node, termed "node 1." Nodes with the same parent are called siblings.

The following diagram shows a data hierarchy.

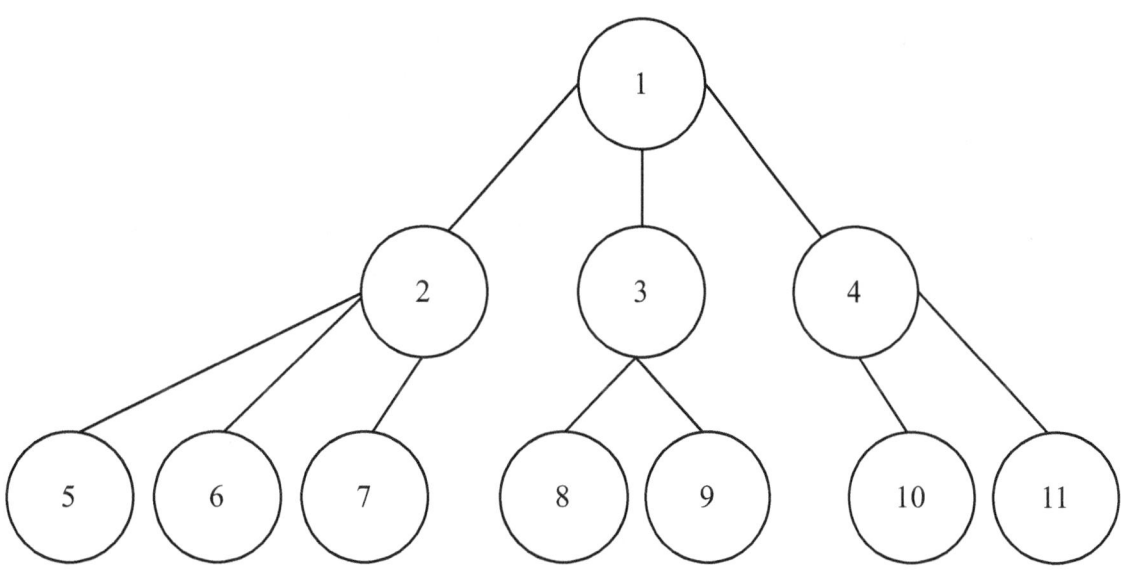

 Organizing Data

A **field** represents a single piece of information. Related fields are grouped together in a **record**. Records are grouped together in a file. For example, the fields "name," "price," "color" and "number in stock" make a product's record. The records of all of the products that a business supplies compose a file.

A **database** consists of related files. A product database, for example, may include the product file and the customer file, as well as the relationships between the two files – for example, what products each customer bought.

Data Query

Queries are used to drive the processing function of the database system to output specific information. Queries can be expressed in several ways, including by example, by form or through structured query language (SQL).

An SQL projection requires the following keywords SELECT and FROM. SELECT tells the system what attributes the user requires as output. An asterisk (*) in the SELECT command indicates that all attributes from the relation should be returned. FROM designates the relation that will provide the input.

In addition to the required keywords, a projection can specify criteria for output using the WHERE command. The ORDER BY keyword is used to tell the system how the output should be arranged. In the ORDER BY command, ASC means "ascending" and DESC means "descending".

The following SQL query would yield a list of all employees hired after January 1, 2005. The list would be in alphabetical order by last name.

```
SELECT      LastName, FirstName
FROM        EMPLOYEE
WHERE       HireDate>1/1/2005
ORDER BY    LastName ASC
```

SQL has a few built-in mathematical functions such as COUNT, SUM and AVG (average).

Data Update

Although many database systems have forms for inserting, deleting or editing records, ns can also be performed using SQL. The syntax INSERT INTO… VALUES is used to place new records.

INSERT   INTO EMPLOYEE
                (EmployeeNumber, LastName, FirstName, HireDate, Department)
                VALUES (156, 'Doe', 'John', 1/1/2004, 'Advertising')

Records can be deleted from the database using the command DELETE… WHERE.

DELETE   EMPLOYEE
WHERE   EMPLOYEE.EmployeeNumber = 156

The UPDATE… SET… WHERE command is used to edit a data record.

UPDATE   EMPLOYEE
SET   LastName = 'Smith'
WHERE   EmployeeNumber = 170

The insert, delete and edit functions can be used on single records or sets of data. If a business were to lay off the entire advertising department, for example, the database administrator might use the following SQL projection:

DELETE   EMPLOYEE
WHERE   EMPLOYEE.Department = 'Advertising'

DBMS

Database Management Systems (DBMS) are used to help organize and analyze the information stored in a database. The user simply inputs a query, which indicates the information that they want displayed, and the system will go through the files in the database to find the answer. For example, libraries that have online catalogs are a type of DBMS. The user, or the person searching for a book, inputs a query, such as the name of the book, and the system searches through the library's records to return all the results that fit the query.

DBMSs can work in many different ways. Two structures through which DBMSs can organize data are the relational model and the hierarchical model. The hierarchical model was one of the earliest models used in databases. It organizes information into parent-child relationships, essentially making a tree of information where one category leads to other categories which leads to other categories. They can only be connected by going up through the levels. Because of this inefficiency relational database structures are now more commonly used. The relational model organizes data into tables. Each table would have a column with the primary information, and any other relevant information that goes along with it. The information is connected to all other tables that contain similar information (which would then also have additional or different information), creating a web rather than a tree.

The problem that naturally arises with relational models is redundancy. Information may be placed in multiple tables or areas which just takes up storage and makes organization more difficult. Because of this problem the practice of normalization evolved. The goal of normalization is to reduce redundancy and ensure that information stored on tables is actually relevant. There are many different levels of organization which build on one another. These range from the First Normal Form (1NF), which includes deleting duplicate information on a table, to the Fourth Normal Form (4NF).

 Information Processing Management

SYSTEM DEVELOPMENT PROCESSES

The development of a business solution using computers is called **information systems development** or **application development**. The major activities are: investigation, analysis, design, implementation, and maintenance. Together this is called the **information systems development cycle** or **life cycle** of the system.

The investigation phase may be called **information systems planning. Strategic planning** deals with policies, strategies and objectives for the information needs of the entire organization. **Operational planning** deals with operating budgets, including budgets for information systems maintenance, upgrade, and new projects. **Project planning** is the first step in developing a new information system and is the first step in the waterfall software development model already discussed.

Part of planning is conducting feasibility studies. A **cost/benefit analysis** projects the costs and potential long-term savings of the system. **Economic feasibility** takes the results of the cost/benefit analysis to determine if the project should continue. **Technical feasibility** determines if the proposed project can actually be accomplished with currently available technology. **Operational feasibility** determines if management and employees will be able to utilize the new system effectively.

The activities of information system development overlap in time. For example, it doesn't matter whether you call the feasibility studies part of the system development or part of the software development. In a particular organization, the difference is primarily in the title of the staff that performs the studies.

TYPES OF INFORMATION PROCESSING APPLICATIONS

Central to any business is the concept of a transaction and a **transaction processing system (TPS)** supports the need of a business to track transactions such as order processing, general ledger, accounts payable and receivable, inventory management, payroll, and data required by law.

Batch processing is not interactive and has its roots in the original mainframe environment of the 1960's. A batch application gathers information over a period of time and records the individual transactions in a file. At routine time intervals (daily, weekly), the file of accumulated transactions is processed against a **master file** that contains the status of each account, for example.

The entire set of transactions is processed, resulting in the update of the entire master file during one batch processing session. A primary concept of batch processing is sorted order. The master file records are stored with a key, like an account number, that is sorted in ascending or descending order. The transaction file is then also sorted into the same order so that the transactions and master records can more easily be matched together. The major disadvantage of batch processing is that the master file is out-of-date between updates and it not responsive to the real-time needs of inquiries.

Real-time processing means that transactions are processed immediately. The familiar **online transaction processing (OLTP)** systems are an example of real-time processing. Files and databases are always up-to-date and no sorting is required. However, additional security and error detection software must be added to real-time systems to prevent instantaneous corruption of the data.

STANDARDS

The world cannot function without standards and the information processing industry is no exception. There are numerous professional and governmental agencies that cooperate to standardize programming languages. For example, the Conference on Data-Systems Languages (**CODASYL**) is the professional organization that is responsible for improving and standardizing COBOL. The **American National Standards Institute (ANSI)** develops standards for all the major programming languages. Groups such as the Internet Engineering Task Force and the World Wide Web Consortium have defined standards for the Internet.

Security and Controls

There are three types of controls for ensuring the security of an information system: information system controls, procedural controls, and physical facility controls.

Information system controls attempt to ensure the accuracy of data and results. **Garbage in/garbage out (GIGO)** means when invalid data is entered the results will also be invalid. Error checking of keyed inputs for range of values and other characteristics or only allowing selections from drop-down input boxes prevents invalid data from entering the system. An **audit trail** provides for tracing the entire processing path of a transaction.

Encryption of data, modifying it so that it cannot be deciphered with the encryption key, is a key method of securing transmitted data. **Decryption** is the restoration of the message to its original form. Data that is not encrypted is called **plaintext** while data that is encrypted is called **ciphertext**. The primary method in use today for data encryption is called **data encryption standard (DES)** which is a secret key form of encryption using one key.

Public key encryption uses two keys: a **public key** that is broadcast and a **private key** that is known to the receiver of the data. Only the receiver can decrypt the message using the private key. The most common public key method is **Rivest-Shamir-Adleman (RSA) encryption**. A **digital signature** is a means of using public key encryption to verify the identity of a sender.

Procedural controls indicate how the operations should be conducted for maximum security. Separation of duties implies that one person does not have sufficient access to the system to corrupt it. Standardized procedures ensure and promote uniformity and guard against errors and fraud.

Verifying that a person who is attempting to access a computer system is an authorized user is an important procedural control and is called **authentication**. The main method used for authentication is the use of a **password**, a series of letters and numbers that presumably are known only between the system and the authorized user. The term **password protection** or **password protected** applies to the system itself, meaning that a password is required to access the system. Individuals who gain unauthorized access to a computer system are called **hackers.**

Biometric controls which measure physical traits of a user such as retina or face scanning are becoming popular. Networks can be made more secure by the addition of a **firewall**, which protects the identity of the network nodes from the outside world of the Internet.

Physical facility controls are methods for protecting the physical plant from damage. Examples are: fire detection systems, emergency power systems, and temperature and-humidity controls. Natural disasters do occur and every organization needs a **disaster recovery plan** which lays out responsibilities and procedures for continuing operations in the event of a disaster. A disaster recovery plan is not the same as a **system recovery plan** which provides for recovering from a major failure of the information processing system.

Personal computers that interact with other computers through a network or electronic mail can be subjected to attack by malicious programs. A **virus** is a program that embeds itself into another program and infects a personal computer when the other program runs. A virus will make copies of itself within other programs as well. A **worm** is a virus that will locate and corrupt data. A **Trojan horse** is a useful program that when installed contains unanticipated code that allows unauthorized collection or destruction of a user's data. The best protection from infection is to periodically run **virus-checking software** that will detect and eliminate known viruses.

Information Processing Careers

The following lists some of the career opportunities available in the information processing realm:

- Chief Information Officer (CIO) – executive director of information systems.
- Operations manager – in charge of the physical operation of computer equipment.
- Computer operator – person who is in charge of overseeing the daily activity of the computers.
- Network manager – in charge of computer network.
- Network specialist or network engineer – a person whose responsibility is to set up and maintain a network.
- Programming manager – in charge of programming activities.
- Analyst – in charge of analysis phases of system or software development and may perform design as well.
- Programmer – person who translates the design into code, performs testing (**debugging** which is removal of errors), and documents the system components.
- Applications programmer – programmer whose job is to develop information systems or application programs.
- Systems programmer – a person who develops, sets up or maintains operating systems.

- Database programmer – a programmer whose specialty is programming interfaces to a data base management system.
- Database administrator (DBA) – person who defines and maintains a database and the data dictionary.

The titles given to individuals who work in information technology (IT) are as varied as the industries that employ them. The above is a sampling of some the most popular titles.

Outsourcing is when a company moves part of their business to another location, generally outside the country which they are located in. For example, it is much cheaper for a company to manufacture their toys in China than it is in the United States. They may choose to outsource their manufacturing to China and have the toys shipped back to the United States for distribution. Another example is that many companies find it cheaper to have their customer service or support call centers in countries other than the United States where a minimum wage is enforced.

In the software industry, India and China are emerging markets which can provide inexpensive technical labor for companies needing help with programming, web design, etc.

Applications in Organizations

MANAGEMENT DECISION MAKING

Managers in business are required to make decisions about their area of responsibility within the organization. Besides providing data in report or graphical form, information applications can provide tools to aid the decision-making process.

Analytical processing applications support decision-making by providing projections, comparisons, statistical inferences and decision analysis tools. A **decision support system (DSS)** and **executive information system (EIS)** are examples of analytical applications.

These applications are comprised of three components: data management, user interface, and model management. A DSS or EIS is based upon a specialized database constructed for data mining. The user interface provides for interactive ad-hoc queries to the database with an emphasis on graphical outputs. A **model** is a computer simulation based upon mathematics or statistics of the real world. In a DSS or EIS, changing values within the model reflect the user's concept of changes in the real-world to analyze "what-if" scenarios.

A **geographic information system (GIS)** integrates a geographic database with the DSS so that analyses can be accomplished, for example, by geographic region. A GIS is capable of producing graphical outputs that contain maps. A GIS may be integrated with a **global positioning system (GPS)** which is capable of pinpointing the location of the unit being tracked anywhere in the world. A **group decision support system (GDSS)** supports the exchange of ideas and opinions within a group or at a meeting. This may include an **electronic meeting system (EMS)**.

A **knowledge-based information system** adds methods from **artificial intelligence (AI)**, a branch of computer science that attempts to endow computers with the ability to make inferences from multiple hypotheses.

An expert system is an application that has been developed using AI methods that have been applied to a highly specific area of knowledge and is capable of giving advice about that area. Expert systems generate answers to questions in their area of expertise and are able to explain the rationale for the answer while performing the problem-solving work. Basically, expert systems are designed to work like a human brain, eliminating the need to consult an expert or professional.

Expert systems are useful and efficient when faced with objective problems, and problems in which human input is unnecessary. For example, an expert system may be useful in diagnosing diseases. They could consider the list of systems, and come up with a disease which would logically be described by them. However, if a business manager wants to know how to increase customer satisfaction ratings, or which of two products would be more popular, it would be more help to have human input, such as through a survey. Benefits of expert systems also include the fact that they don't require salaries and are easily and quickly reproduced, whereas it takes years for a human to become an expert on a subject. However, expert systems can only "think" through formulaic approaches.

They can have all the information in the world, but do not necessarily have the ability to think creatively. They think in set processes and through set rules, again showing that though useful in many situations there are situations in which human reactions are useful as well. For example, a business might have an expert system and if an employee has a problem with the printer or another machine it would ask questions and give advice as to what might be wrong. On the other hand, a computer software company which is trying to come up with a new piece of innovative software wouldn't be able to use an expert system to do this for them, because expert systems work with existing data and information.

USER APPLICATIONS

Word processing software allows the user to create, edit, revise and print text material and to produce documents. These applications provide an editor for working on the text, a formatting program for producing documents, a dictionary, a thesaurus, a spelling and grammar checker, integrated graphics and a mail-merge capability.

Mail merges are used in creating large amounts of documents which are essentially the same, but which have unique elements. For example, colleges often send out letters to perspective applicants. Each letter has identical information, but a different person's name at the beginning. A mail merge would be used to accomplish this. Mail merges can also be used in print labels, or addresses on envelopes. To create a mail merge, a person writes the main document with all of the identical elements and leaves placeholders where the unique elements will go. These fields could look like:

{first name} {last name}
{address}
{address2}
{city}, {state} {zip}

Then a data file is created and linked with the main document and the computer does the rest. Mail merges are usually performed in programs like Microsoft Word or WordPerfect.

Desktop publishing software provides the next level of sophistication in supporting the layout of newsletters, announcements, and advertising copy.

Spreadsheets are made up of intersecting rows and columns. The columns are listed alphabetically, the first being A, the second B, the third C and so on. The rows are listed numerically, the first being 1, the second 2, the third 3 and so on. The areas where a column and row intersect are called cells. Each cell is named according to the row and column it falls under. For example, the cell in the first row and first column is called cell A1. A cell in the fourth column and thirtieth row would be called D30.

Spreadsheet software allows the user to create a traditional spreadsheet or grid of rows and columns that can be tallied automatically and formatted in to reports or viewed graphically. An example of spreadsheet software would be Excel.

Graphics software supports the production of graphs, maps and drawings. **Presentation graphics software** contains presentation templates, multiple fonts, drawing tools, spelling checker, and possibly a library of clip art.

Speech recognition software recognizes human voice messages. **Discrete speech recognition** can recognize only one word at a time while **continuous speech recognition** recognizes normal speaking. Programs come with vocabularies of 30,000 to 75,000 words.

OFFICE SYSTEMS

Electronic mail (E-mail) is the sending and receiving of messages through a network. Users receive their messages after they log on to the network. An e-mail message can be broadcast to multiple users or to an entire mailing list. **Voice mail** stores digitized voice messages. **Facsimile (fax)** capabilities can be integrated into personal computers, allowing a message to be sent from the computer to any fax machine.

Electronic meeting systems (EMS) allow meetings and conferences to be held when participants are located in different physical locations. **Teleconferencing** is an electronic meeting that is supported by closed circuit television broadcasting.

The above applications are components of **office automation systems**. These systems improve productivity by streamlining the flow of documents and messages among co-workers. **Work group computing** supports cooperative work. Other terms for work group computing are **computer-supported collaboration (CSC), computer-based systems for collaborative work (CSCW)**, or **collaborative work support systems (CWSS)**. People working together as a group do not need to be in the same physical location. It is advantageous for the group to use the same suite of support programs because the bundling of software applications lowers the cost of purchase; programs in the suite work together; data and procedures can easily be shared amongst users while the organization maximizes its investment by using the full functionality of the suite.

Internet and the World Wide Web

The **Internet** is a network of computer networks. The Internet has its origins in AR-PANET, a U.S. Department of Defense network that began in 1969. The Internet is composed of **Internet service providers (ISP's)** that provide network services to en-dusers for typically a monthly fee. Some ISPs are **backbone networks** that exist solely to connect the major networks of the other service providers.

Information on the Internet is transmitted as **packets.** A packet contains the sending and receiving addresses for the information and its sequence within the message. Individual packets comprising a message may take different routes over the network on their way to the receiving computer and the message is reassembled when all the packets arrive. The protocol or standardized set of rules for transmitting packets is called **Internet protocol (IP)**. Another protocol used in conjunction with IP is **transport control protocol (TCP)**. Taken together, these protocols are known as **TCP/IP protocol**.

Every computer that accesses the Internet is given an **IP address** which is four sets of numbers separated by dots, for example, 153.26.128.19. In addition, commercially used computers can have a **domain name** which is more like natural language. The domain name begins with www. and may have multiple parts separated by dots. However, standards exist for what the final part means and the most prevalent suffixes are as follows: .com for commercial sites; .edu for educational sites; .mil for military sites; .gov for government sites; .org for organizations or associations.

The Internet provides three main services: communication services such as electronic mail using simple mail transfer protocol (SMTP), newsgroups, chat rooms, and Internet telephone service; information retrieval services like gopher and file transfer protocol (FTP); and the World Wide Web (WWW). Another type of communication service is **streaming audio and video** that allows the user to hear and see the information as it is transmitted instead of waiting for packets to arrive.

Numerous information retrieval services are available through the Internet. **File transfer protocol (FTP)** provides access to a remote computer for retrieval of files. **Archie** is a software tool that allows a user to search for files at a remote computer. A **gopher** is another software tool that allows users to locate other linked gopher files on Internet servers; users move from site to site searching for information at will. **Electronic Data Interchange (EDI)** is a standard for the electronic exchange of business documents such as invoices and purchase orders.

The World Wide Web is not the same as the Internet. The Internet is the network that transports packets while the World Wide Web is a computer application (software) that uses the network. Another application that uses the Internet is electronic mail. Anyone wishing to offer information through the World Wide Web must establish a **home page** on their **web site**.

Every web site is identified by a **uniform resource locator (URL)**. Most URL's begin with **HTTP** which stands for **hypertext transfer protocol**, the transfer protocol for defining how messages are formatted and transmitted on the Web. The URL specifies the domain name of the web site possibly followed by the page identifier within the web site.

A **browser** or **Web browser** is a program that allows the user to navigate the World Wide Web. **Surfing** is the term given to exploring the links on the web in search of interesting information. A **search engine** is a program that allows the user to enter a word or phrase and the software returns a list of links to web sites that contain that word or phrase. Search engines locate web pages through registration, whereby the creator of the web site informs the search engine of its existence or through the use of a web crawler. A **web crawler** is an application that traverses the web automatically collecting links to be used later by the search engine. A **metasearch engine** submits a query to multiple search engines simultaneously.

With the widespread availability of the Internet, abuses have appeared. Junk e-mail is sent to users who have not requested any information through what is called **spamming**. Sending obscene or abusive e-mail is called **flaming**.

Social and Ethical Issues

The latest trends in information systems, especially on-line e-commerce, have increased the profitability of many businesses. The increases in sales and productivity have continued to support the costs of investments in improved technology. Information systems have had a positive economic impact for business. This may or may not be the case for the individual worker whose job may have been replaced by technology. For the worker, the skill level needed to earn a living has increased.

Privacy is a key issue with regard to the proliferation of information systems and databases that store massive amounts of data about each individual. With the ability to link databases and to mine data warehouses, a vast of amount of information can be obtained about an individual. **Electronic surveillance,** monitoring of a person's activities while using the Internet, is possible and may be a major problem according to the American Civil Liberties Union (ACLU).

Accuracy of information is another issue. While there is the problem of accuracy of an individual's data, there is a broader problem concerning the accuracy of disseminated information. People tend to believe what they see on their television or computer. Publishers of print media have been held accountable for the accuracy of what they place in print but no one verifies the accuracy of what is placed in web sites.

Intellectual property, the intangible property in writing, is usually protected by copyright. Copyright problems exist for both software and the written word when it comes to the Internet. The Internet freely provides many items of intellectual property that were once sold.

Public domain refers to creative works not protected by intellectual property rights, such as copyright, trademark, or patent laws. These works are available for anyone to use, modify, or distribute without seeking permission or paying royalties. Once a work enters the public domain, it becomes part of the shared cultural heritage and is freely accessible to the public.

One common way for a work to enter the public domain is through the expiration of its copyright. In most countries, copyright protection lasts for a certain period, typically the author's life plus a specified number of years after their death. For example, in the United States, works published before 1923 are generally considered to be in the public domain. Famous examples of public domain works include Shakespeare's plays, Beethoven's symphonies, and Jane Austen's novels.

In addition to works whose copyrights have expired, certain types of content are not eligible for copyright protection and automatically fall into the public domain. These include mathematical and scientific formulas, laws, and facts. For instance, Einstein's famous equation, $E=mc^2$, is in the public domain, as are the laws of gravity and thermodynamics. This ensures that scientific knowledge and discoveries can be freely shared and built upon by others.

Government works, such as legal documents, public records, and official reports, are also typically in the public domain. This allows citizens to access and use this information without restrictions. Examples include U.S. Supreme Court decisions, congressional reports, and NASA's space images.

Ondividual words, letters, and symbols are not subject to copyright protection. This is why dictionaries and alphabets are in the public domain, ensuring that language remains a shared resource for all to use.

The public domain provides an essential foundation for creativity, innovation, and the dissemination of knowledge. Artists, writers, and scholars can draw inspiration from and build upon the works of their predecessors without the need for permission or fear of infringing on intellectual property rights. For example, many modern adaptations of classic literature, such as the numerous retellings of "Pride and Prejudice" or "Sherlock Holmes" stories, are possible because the original works are in the public domain.

The public domain encompasses a vast array of creative works freely available for public use, including those whose copyrights have expired and those ineligible for copyright protection. From classic literature and musical compositions to scientific discoveries and government documents, the public domain is a rich resource for creators, researchers, and the general public.

Careers and jobs have changed since the introduction of information systems. Job content has changed in many industries as more and more workers perform their jobs through a computerized workstation. Some people consider working with computers all day as a dehumanizing experience. Some feel that commerce is becoming impersonal.

With increased productivity, workers have more responsibilities and with instantaneous transactions, the pace of work has increased. Both of these factors contribute to job stress. Repetitive strain injuries such as carpal tunnel syndrome have increased. As information systems proliferate, designers will need to include job design and ergonomics (human factors engineering) as factors in the design of the system.

Software Licensing

A software license defines any limitations on how consumers can use a program or application. The license may limit the purpose for which consumers can use the program, how many copies consumers can make for their personal use, the process consumers can use to sell their copies of the software, and the modifications consumers can make to the software. Software users may have to agree to the terms of the software license before they can access all of the functions of a computer program or application.

The two main categories of software licenses are open source licenses and proprietary licenses. These types of licenses differ in how they define the ownership of the software copies.

Open source licenses grant the ownership of a copy of software to the end-user. As a result, the consumer of an open source licensed application usually has the right to change, copy, and distribute the software with few or no restrictions. Under proprietary software licenses, the publisher is the legal owner of the software and the consumer owns only a license to use the software.

Under both proprietary and open source licenses, the designer or publisher retains ownership of the software's copyright. Because they do not own the copyright, end-users are usually prohibited from taking credit for the software. In addition, open source licenses may place restrictions on how users must document and distribute changes they make to the software.

Safety and Security for Networks

Businesses and organizations need to implement network security protocols in order to protect their data from accidents and malicious attacks, and to comply with federal, local, or industry-specific regulations.

Networks consist of connected computers, or "nodes." Network security involves controlling who accesses information at each node and as the information travels between the nodes. A network security system has established access rights that define which users or devices are allowed to complete certain functions. Authentication is the process of identifying users and devices, and verifying that they have the required access rights before data is released.

If a computer network is connected to the Internet or to another network, the external connection can be especially vulnerable. A firewall can be installed in the network to inspect data before it travels into or out of the network. The firewall software or hardware functions by denying access to suspicious data.

Mobile Networks

Amobile network is any network whose nodes are connected using wireless technology. For this reason, mobile networks are often called "wireless networks." The nodes of a mobile network may include computers, output devices such as printers, and cellular telephones. These nodes communicate with each other through electromagnetic waves.

The main advantage of a wireless network over a traditional, line-based configuration is portability. Users are able to leave their desk and still access the network. In addition, wireless connections can allow networks to be configured into arrangements that would have been awkward or impossible to implement using traditional connections.

Mobile networks have several drawbacks. Because users do not have to be physically connected to the network to intercept the communication waves, wireless networks are more vulnerable to security breeches. In addition, data flow rate can be significantly reduced over wireless connections. Because there are several different wireless networking standards, linking nodes from different manufacturers or adding new nodes to an existing network can lead to compatibility problems.

Satellite Transmissions

Satellites use electromagnetic waves to transmit data. These waves travel at over 300 million meters per second (the speed of light), which is why they are able to transmit data so quickly. The types of waves most commonly used for satellites are radio waves and micro waves, depending on the type of data being transmitted. Dish satellites use radio waves, as do GPS satellites. The reason for this is because while some types of electromagnetic waves are absorbed into the atmosphere, radio waves are not.

 Software Life Cycle

Developing software requires eight steps: requirements definition, requirements analysis, preliminary design, detailed design, implementation, system testing, acceptance testing and maintenance.

In the requirements definition phase, the needs of the end user are considered and a list of software specifications is created. The requirements the software will need to fulfill in order to be considered successful are documented. Some important considerations in determining completion of this step include reviewing the document with the customer or user, and checking to make sure all the requirements are considered.

It is also important to consider whether it would cost more to move on and remember something later that needed to be added, or if it would cost more to put off moving on and extending the requirements definition phase. It is also important that too much time isn't spent in this one phase either, as it is possible that the requirements will change while work is being done on the project. Also, the requirements are considered more in depth in the requirements analysis phase.

After the requirements have been defined, it proceeds to the requirements analysis phase where the programming team reviews the software requirements to make sure they are complete and sufficient to meet the end users' needs. The team also makes sure there are sufficient economical, technical, and operational resources available to create software that fulfills the requirements.

For example, the programmers will want to consider the scope of the project, or what exactly it is that is supposed to be accomplished. They will also want to consider the time frame for the project. For example, if a group of programmers is being paid to develop software it is likely that it will need to be completed by a certain date, and they need to know if they will be able to so. Once these things have been determined, the preliminary design phase begins.

In the preliminary design phase, programmers develop different approaches to meet the software requirements. The cost, advantages and disadvantages of each approach are studied and the best option is selected. User interfaces are created and algorithms are developed for high level processes.

Algorithms are the specific processes and instructions that a computer uses to carry out a function, making them essential to the program. To do this the team must decide on a programming language that is well suited to code the algorithms.

Essentially, in this phase the programmers design the basic structure of the program, without any of the intricate details. Because this step involves the structure of the program, it involves the most complex parts to be created. As they go along, the programmers should check periodically to make sure that the program will work to satisfy all of the designated requirements and that it will function well. It is important to understand that in this phase the programmers do not actually create the software, they create the instructions for the functions that it will carry out.

During the detailed design phase, the preliminary design is further developed. All input and output screens and files are designed. Subroutines and subprograms are defined and algorithms needed to process information at these levels are written. Once the software is designed, the software project can move into the implementation phase. At this point, the software has not truly been written yet. Rather, the individual elements of it have all been created.

The implementation phase is when the programmers actually write the software. By using the programming language chosen in the preliminary design phase, code is written to process information according to the algorithms defined in the design phases. As each unit of code is produced, it is tested by itself and in combination with related units. Once the system is coded, reviewed and tested, it is incorporated into the appropriate system where it can be used. A draft of the software documentation is developed throughout this phase.

The system testing phase involves evaluating the software in a setting similar to how it will be used by the end users. All capabilities of the software are tested by members of the programming team. If errors are identified, they are documented and corrected. The system testing phase continues until the software is shown to meet all of the defined requirements without error.

The software documentation is reviewed and edited. In the acceptance testing phase, the software is subjected to further testing. This time, the tests are conducted by people outside the software programming team in order to minimize the possibility of testing bias. If errors are found during the acceptance testing phase, they are corrected by the programming team and the software is tested for further problems. When all identified errors have been corrected and the software passes all testing, a final version of the software documentation is written. The software is considered ready to be employed by the end user.

The last phase of the software life cycle is the maintenance and operations phase. This phase continues for as long as the software is in use. During the maintenance and operations phase, the software is updated to ensure correctness and efficiency.

Programming Methodology

Programming methodology is the process of coding software. Before programming can begin, the interfaces, screens, processes, storage files, and outputs for the software should be defined.

Programmers write units of code to produce the interfaces, screens, processes, storage files, and outputs that will compose the software. Each unit is tested individually. As units are completed, they are combined into related functional groups called modules. Each module is also tested to make sure the units are compatible.

As modules are finished, they are connected to produce subsystems. Eventually, all of the modules are integrated to create the complete software. Each time a module is added, the system is tested so that problems with newly added components can be identified.

At each step of the programming process, the software is documented and reviewed. A protocol for testing the completed software is designed.

Designing software is usually performed top-down. This means that the functional requirements for and relationships between every module is defined before the individual algorithms are designed. Programming, however, usually proceeds from the bottom-up, with individual algorithms coded and tested before they are combined into modules, and modules constructed and tested before they are integrated into subsystems. Only after all of the subsystems have been shown to work properly are they joined to create the complete program.

Data Types and Algorithms

An algorithm is a set of instructions for performing a specific task. An algorithm must use a measurable amount of resources and be completed within a definite time. The instructions within an algorithm must be clear and unambiguous. Algorithms can be written using mathematical signs, Boolean logic operators, programming languages, or a pseudo language. Algorithms can not result in endless loops, continue for an infinite amount of time, or use infinite resources.

A data type is a set of data values along with operations associated with those values. Examples of data types include real numbers, integers, characters, strings, and pointers.

An abstract data type (ADT) is a data type whose definition is not dependent on how it is used by any particular program. A simple ADT is the stack. In a stack, the last data saved is the first data returned. The name "stack" comes from the visualization of the data as a stack of trays, where the tray most recently placed on the stack is on the top and therefore the first to be taken off. Operations associated with a stack include "push," which is used to add a new data element to the stack, and "pop," which returns the most recent element.

The data elements involved in a stack can be integers, strings, pointers, or any other data type including other stacks. Because the definitions for the operations associated with a stack do not depend on what type of data is being stored in the stack, a stack is an ADT.

Another commonly used ADT is the queue. Where a stack accesses data on a "first in, last out" (FILO) basis, a queue is a "first in, first out" (FIFO) structure. The first element added to the queue is the first one that can be accessed. The operators "push" and "pop" are also used on queue structures.

Arrays are data structures whose elements can be accessed by reference to the array name and the position of the element within the array. Arrays can of one or multiple dimensions. In single dimension arrays, an element is accessed using the array name and a single integer that identifies the element's place within the array. The following single dimension array has four integer elements.

$ARR = [1,3,5,7]$

A programmer could call on any element within the array by referencing the element's position within ARR. In this example, ARR(1) = 1, ARR(2) = 3, ARR(3) = 5, and ARR(4) = 7. Subscripts can also be used to indicate an elements position within an array.

In multidimensional arrays, an element is accessed using the array name and an ordered set of integers. The number of integers required to identify a particular element of an array is called that array's dimension. In arrays of dimension two, the ordered pair used to identify an element lists the row number first and then the column number as shown in the example below.

$$ARR = \begin{vmatrix} 1 & 3 & 5 \\ 7 & 9 & 2 \\ 4 & 6 & 8 \end{vmatrix}$$

ARR(1,1) = 1; ARR(1,2) = 3. ARR(1,3) = 5; ARR(2,1) = 7; ARR(2,2) = 9; ARR(2,3) = 2; ARR(3,1) = 4; ARR(3,2) = 6; ARR(3,3) = 8.

 Programming Concepts

Although computer languages differ in how they implement operations and data structures, there are several concepts common to every language.

Regardless of the language used, programs rely on variables for temporary storage of numbers, characters, and other data types. A variable is used to hold data that is inputted or calculated at one point in an algorithm and will be outputted or further processed later in the algorithm.

There are two types of variables: global and local. Global variables are in scope, or able to be read and modified, throughout the entire program. Local variables are only in scope for a defined part of the program, such as a function or subroutine. Although the variable itself can not be accessed or changed by parts of the program for which the local variable is not in scope, the value of the variable can be passed to other functions or subroutines.

Programmers use loops to tell the computer to follow a list of instructions multiple times. A loop can be a condition, counted, or infinite. In a condition loop, the computer checks a variable or set of variables against a defined condition. If the variables pass the condition test, the instructions within the loop are performed. After each completion of the loop, the condition is checked again. When the variables fail the condition test, the instructions within the loop are not carried out and the loop ends. Consider the following simple loop:

WHILE X > 0
LOOP
X=X-1
END LOOP

If X=5 at the start of the loop, the loop would be completed five times. After the fifth iteration, X would equal 0. The condition test would not be passed and the instructions within the loop would not be carried out.

The terms WHILE or UNTIL in a program indicate a condition loop.

A counted loop is one that is performed a set number of times. In many higher level programming languages, the terms FOR and NEXT are used to create a counted loop. The FOR statement is used to create a counter. NEXT instructs the computer to advance the counter by one. The following counted loop would be repeated five times.

```
FOR X=1 to 5
        A=A+1
        B=B+1
NEXT
```

By defining a counting variable before the loop, a counted loop can be written as a condition loop. The following conditional loop is equivalent to the counted loop sample above:

```
X=1
WHILE X<6
LOOP
        A=A+1
        B=B+1
X=X+1 END LOOP
```

Sometimes, either by design or through error, a loop may be repeated until the computer turns off or an error closes the program. Loops that do not end by themselves are called endless or infinite loops. The following pseudocode is an example of an endless loop. The condition that signals the start of the loop is always true.

```
X=1
WHILE X>0
LOOP
        A=A+1
        B=B+1
X=X+1
END LOOP
```

Logic Concepts

Computer algorithms use logic conditions to define how to treat data. Logic conditions are used to test data then carry out instructions based on the results of the test. Some common tests performed on data include:

- Equals (= or ==): The data being tested is equal to the value of a given static or variable.
- Not equals (!=): The data being tested does not equal the value of a given static or variable.

- Less than (<): The data being tested has a lower value than that of a given static or variable.
- Greater than (>): The data being tested has a higher value than that of a given static or variable.

In most circumstances, the data being tested must be compared to a static or variable of the same data type. Some programming languages will automatically convert the type of the data being tested if it does not match the comparison data. For example, if the program compares a character to an integer, the character may be converted into an integer based on its ASCII value.

More complicated tests can be performed using logical, also called Boolean, operators to relate data. The Boolean operators are and (&&), or (||), and not (!).

Logic tests are performed using the IF statement and variations of the IF statement. The syntax used to code an IF statement is dependant on the computer language used. However it is coded, and IF statement follows a basic process:

IF (the result of a logic test is true) THEN (do action X)

The following table shows some simple logic tests using test data A and a given variable B.

IF Statement Logic Tests

Symbolic Representation	Explanation
IF A=B, THEN Y	If A equals B, then do action Y
IF A!=B, THEN Y	If A does not equal B, then do action Y
IF A>B, THEN Y	If A is greater than B, then do action Y
IF A>||=B, THEN Y	If A is greater than or equal to B, then do action Y
IF A<B, THEN Y	If A is less than B, then do action Y
IF A<||=B, THEN Y	If A is less than or equal to B, then do action Y
IF A=0 || B=0, THEN Y	If A equals 0 or B equals zero, then do action Y
IF A=0 && B=0, THEN Y	If A equals zero and B equals zero, then do action Y

There are three common variations to the IF statement: ELSE, ELSE IF, and CASE. The ELSE statement defines an alternative action to take if the test fails.

IF (the result of a logic test is true) THEN (do action X) ELSE (do action Y)

ELSE IF provides the rules for an additional test if the previous test fails.

IF (the result of a logic test is true) THEN (do action X)
ELSE IF (the results of the a different logic test are true) THEN (do action Z)

CASE statements are used to provide action rules for tests with several outcomes.

>CASE 1: Do action X
>CASE 2: Do action Y
>CASE 3: Do action Z

A CASE statement is the equivalent to a series of ELSE IF statements. The example CASE statement above can be rewritten using ELSE IF commands.

>IF (the result of logic test 1 is true) THEN (do action X)
>ELSE IF (the result of logic test 2 is true) THEN (do action Y)
>ELSE IF (the result of logic test 3 is true) THEN (do action Z)

CASE statements are sometimes called SELECT or SWITCH statements.

Software Development Tools

Software development tools are essential applications that streamline the programming process and make it easier for developers to create, test, and maintain software. These tools automate repetitive and time-consuming tasks, facilitate complex functions, and help programmers work more efficiently. Four most commonly used software development tools are compilers, debuggers, documentation generators, and integrated development environments (IDEs).

Compilers are software tools that translate code written in one programming language into another. This is particularly important for programs written in high-level languages like C++, Java, or Python, which need to be translated into lower-level languages such as assembly or machine language before the computer can execute them. While it is possible to compile code manually, the process is incredibly complex, error-prone, and time-consuming. Compilers automate this process, making it much faster and more accurate. For example, the GNU Compiler Collection (GCC) is a widely used compiler that supports multiple programming languages, including C, C++, and Fortran.

Debuggers are software development tools that help programmers identify and fix errors in their code. They allow developers to step through lines of code one at a time, track the values of variables, and locate instructions that cause crashes or unexpected behavior. This makes it much easier for programmers to pinpoint the source of a problem and correct it quickly. Popular debuggers include GDB (GNU Debugger) for Unix-like systems and the Visual Studio Debugger for Windows.

Documentation generators are tools that automatically create user guides and programming documentation based on information about the design and implementation of an application. These tools can significantly speed up documentation by gathering relevant information from screens, forms, source code files, and data flow diagrams. This saves time and ensures that the documentation is accurate and up-to-date. Doxygen is a well-known documentation generator that supports multiple programming languages and can generate documentation in various formats, such as HTML, LaTeX, and PDF.

Integrated Development Environments (IDEs) are comprehensive software development tools that provide a unified interface for writing, testing, and debugging code. IDEs typically include syntax highlighting, code completion, version control integration, and built-in debuggers. By combining multiple development tools into a single interface, IDEs can significantly boost programmer productivity and reduce the need to switch between different applications. Popular IDEs include Microsoft Visual Studio for Windows, Xcode for macOS, and Eclipse, which supports multiple platforms and programming languages.

To illustrate the use of these tools, consider a software developer working on a large C++ project. They would start by writing their code in an IDE like Visual Studio, which provides features like syntax highlighting and code completion to help them write code more quickly and accurately. Once the code is written, they would use a compiler like GCC to translate it into machine language that can be executed by the computer.

If the developer encounters any issues with their code, they can use a debugger like GDB to step through the program line by line, examining variables and identifying the source of the problem. Once the code is working correctly, they can use a documentation generator like Doxygen to automatically create user guides and API references based on comments in the source code.

In summary, software development tools like compilers, debuggers, documentation generators, and IDEs are essential for modern software development. They automate tedious and error-prone tasks, help developers work more efficiently, and ultimately lead to faster development cycles and higher-quality software.

 ## Sample Test Questions

Test questions are an additional way to learn the material for your test. All the questions and answers that follow may not necessarily be covered in the previously in the study guide. However, this is information that you will need to know for the test. If you are unfamiliar with the answer make a note of it so you can make sure to memorize that topic.

1) A gigabyte equals how many bytes?

   A) One thousand
   B) Ten thousand
   C) One million
   D) One billion
   E) One trillion

The correct answer is D:) One billion.

2) What type of software allows tracking of costs, time lines and events related to projects?

   A) Presentation
   B) Project management
   C) CAD
   D) RAD
   E) Report

The correct answer is B:) Project management.

3) A high school senior is graduating. She writes and addresses 100 graduation announcements by hand. This work could have been completed quicker through the use of a(n)

   A) Processing system
   B) Mail merge
   C) Public domain
   D) TCP/IP
   E) Interpreter

The correct answer is B:) Mail merge. She could have made labels to speed up the process. This situation would be perfect for a mail merge.

4) An 8 bit video card can display how many colors?

   A) 8
   B) 16
   C) 64
   D) 256
   E) 512

The correct answer is D:) 256.

5) Which job function oversees the timeliness, budget and schedule of a project?

   A) Project manager
   B) Software engineer
   C) Network administrator
   D) Data analyst
   E) Beta tester

The correct answer is A:) Project manager.

6) In which of the following situations would it be plagiarism to quote Kepler's laws of planetary motion?

   A) A student writing a science report about the elliptical orbits of planets.
   B) A scientist calculating the orbit of the planet Neptune.
   C) An English teacher mentioning the equations during a class discussion.
   D) A physics major completing an assignment dealing with planetary motion.
   E) None of the above

The correct answer is E:) None of the above. Scientific laws, such as Kepler's laws of planetary motion, are public domain and it is always acceptable to use and quote them.

7) URL stands for

   A) Ultimate Resource Location
   B) Ultimate Relation Location
   C) Uniform Resource Locator
   D) Uniform Relation Locator
   E) Uniform Relative Locator

The correct answer is C:) Uniform Resource Locator.

8) What type of software converts handwriting to text on the computer?

   A) OCR
   B) MICR
   C) Biometric device
   D) ORC
   E) Font scanner

The correct answer is A:) OCR.

9) Items with a "Made in China" label were

   A) Insourced
   B) Private domain
   C) Outsourced
   D) Wireless
   E) None of the above

The correct answer is C:) Outsourced. If they were made in China, then the company must have sent them there to be manufactured and returned them to the United States for distribution.

10) Which of the following is NOT an image file type?

   A) GIF
   B) BMP
   C) JPEG
   D) PSD
   E) JOT

The correct answer is E:) JOT.

11) Screen resolution is described in units of

   A) Inches
   B) Centimeters
   C) Nanometers
   D) Pixels
   E) VPNs

The correct answer is D:) Pixels.

12) Which of the following is an output device?

   A) Printer
   B) Mouse
   C) Keyboard
   D) Scanner
   E) Fax

The correct answer is A:) Printer.

13) POS terminals are found everywhere BUT the following?

   A) Grocery store
   B) Gift shop
   C) Clothing store
   D) Office building
   E) Auto parts store

The correct answer is D:) Office building.

14) What word below is part of a mathematical formula to encrypt information?

   A) Hash
   B) Encode
   C) Macro
   D) Password
   E) Key code

The correct answer is A:) Hash.

15) The intersection on a spreadsheet of the fifth row and the second column is called

   A) Box B5
   B) Box E2
   C) Cell B5
   D) Cell B2
   E) Cell 52

The correct answer is C:) Cell B5. The rows are listed numerically and the columns alphabetically. Additionally, the intersections are called cells.

16) Which job function creates and codes computer applications?

    A) Project manager
    B) Software engineer
    C) Network administrator
    D) Data analyst
    E) Beta tester

The correct answer is B:) Software engineer.

17) Which job function works with the engineers to create documentation for the product?

    A) Graphic designer
    B) Desktop publisher
    C) Technical writer
    D) Analyst
    E) Project manager

The correct answer is C:) Technical writer.

18) Which of the following would NOT be used in association with a MIDI device?

    A) Keyboard
    B) Speakers
    C) Scanner
    D) Software
    E) Musical instruments

The correct answer is C:) Scanner.

19) A programmer writes a program in C++. In order to understand it, the computer uses a program to translate it into binary code. The program that does this is called a(n)

    A) Translator
    B) Compiler
    C) Interpreter
    D) Interchange device
    E) None of the above

The correct answer is B:) Compiler. Compilers translate information into machine language.

20) Electronic components that make up the computer such as the monitor are called?

   A) Hardware
   B) Software
   C) CPU
   D) Desktop
   E) Recycle bin

The correct answer is A:) Hardware.

21) Which of the following is an input device?

   A) Keyboard
   B) Monitor
   C) Printer
   D) Power supply
   E) Chair

The correct answer is A:) Keyboard.

22) What allows information to be more closely packed on blu ray discs than DVDs?

   A) The information on DVDs is encoded in a more complex manner than on blu ray discs.
   B) Blu ray discs are read with a blue laser, whereas DVDs are read with a red laser.
   C) DVDs are created out of a different material than blu ray discs.
   D) Blu ray discs are read with a red laser, whereas DVDs are read with a blue laser.
   E) The information isn't more closely packed. Blu ray discs are just twice as big as DVDs.

The correct answer is B:) Blu ray discs are read with a blue laser, whereas DVDs are read with a red laser.

23) An example of a biometric device is

   A) Fingerprint scanner
   B) Optical mouse
   C) Infrared
   D) Body language sensor
   E) Speech access

The correct answer is A:) Fingerprint scanner.

24) What type of electromagnetic waves are used in satellite transmission?

   A) Infrared
   B) Micro
   C) Gamma
   D) Radio
   E) Ultra Violet

The correct answer is D:) Radio. Radio waves are useful because they are not absorbed in to the atmosphere when they pass through it.

25) A master control program the oversees all the functions of the computer is called?

   A) OS
   B) ALU
   C) RAM
   D) ROM
   E) CD-ROM

The correct answer is A:) OS.

26) A manager needs to make a business decision. To help them compile and interpret information they may use a(n)

   A) GUI
   B) LAN
   C) GUI
   D) HTML
   E) DSS

The correct answer is E:) DSS. This stands for Decision Support System.

27) Which device can information NOT be read from and re-written?

   A) ROM
   B) RAM
   C) Floppy disk
   D) Thumb drive
   E) Disk drive

The correct answer is A:) ROM.

28) When a document is transferred from one computer to another, what is used?

   A) GUI
   B) RAM
   C) FTP
   D) HTML
   E) LAN

The correct answer is C:) FTP. This stands for File Transfer Protocol.

29) Someone who tries to illegally access your computer files would be called a

   A) Sniffer
   B) Mummy
   C) Hacker
   D) Caster
   E) Tracker

The correct answer is C:) Hacker.

30) Four computers are networked together by being directly connected through a small box. The box is called a

   A) LAN
   B) WAN
   C) Token ring
   D) Hub
   E) ERM

The correct answer is D:) Hub.

31) What is the component that supports the standard arithmetic function like add and subtract as well as logical operations alike AND and OR?

   A) CPU
   B) DOS
   C) ALU
   D) RISC
   E) CISC

The correct answer is C:) ALU.

32) Which of the following is a computer language used in designing web pages?

   A) HTML
   B) GUI
   C) LAN
   D) TCP/IP
   E) OLTP

The correct answer is A:) HTML. This stands for Hyper Text Markup Language.

33) The reverse of downloading information is called

   A) Streaming
   B) Flowing
   C) Outsourcing
   D) Uploading
   E) Sharing

The correct answer is D:) Uploading.

34) A group of friends get together and manually connect their computers with cables to play a game. The network they created is called a

   A) GUI
   B) WAN
   C) Hub
   D) LAN
   E) TCP/IP

The correct answer is D:) LAN. This stands for Local Area Network.

35) A beta version of software is created for

   A) Purchase by end users
   B) Scientists
   C) Programmers
   D) Testing by end users
   E) Second editions

The correct answer is D:) Testing by end users.

36) A business starts up in one city. Soon, they have offices in nearby cities as well. The computers in the different offices are all linked through the company's

   A) LAN
   B) FTP
   C) TCP/IP
   D) HTML
   E) WAN

The correct answer is E:) WAN. Wide Area Networks can cover large areas, such as across or between cities.

37) How many bits are in a byte?

   A) 1
   B) 2
   C) 4
   D) 8
   E) 10

The correct answer is D:) 8.

38) Binary-coded decimals are stored as ____-bit binary number.

   A) 1
   B) 2
   C) 3
   D) 4
   E) 5

The correct answer is D:) 4.

39) Which of the following statements is TRUE?

   A) In a token ring topology, all computers are connected to a central hub.
   B) In token rings, all of the computers are connected in a large circle.
   C) Token ring topology is typically used to connect multiple WANs.
   D) Token ring topology is beneficial because it allows all computers to communicate simultaneously.
   E) None of the above

The correct answer is B:) In token rings, all of the computers are connected in a large circle. A token then passes through the network allowing the transmission of data.

40) What is "electronic conferencing"?

   A) A combination of videoconferencing and whiteboard conferencing
   B) Meetings between group member who are in the same room at the same time, but in separate workspaces where they can key in comments on a common document
   C) Conferencing through a computer network
   D) Viewing the same document at different locations
   E) None of the above

The correct answer is A:) A combination of videoconferencing and whiteboard conferencing.

41) Which would not be a typical accuracy control used in a transaction processing system (TSP)?

   A) Control totals
   B) Security systems
   C) Audit trails
   D) Backup procedures
   E) None of the above

The correct answer is B:) Security systems.

42) Which of the following is NOT an example of metadata?

   A) The .doc on the end of a file name used to describe the type of file.
   B) A summary of the information found on a webpage.
   C) A description of the size and designer of an image on a webpage.
   D) A spreadsheet which contains a record of a company's sales.
   E) None of the above

The correct answer is D:) A spreadsheet which contains a record of a company's sales. This would be data, not metadata.

43) A kilobyte equals how many bytes?

   A) 10000 bytes
   B) 10240 bytes
   C) 1000 bytes
   D) 1024 bytes
   E) None of the above

The correct answer is D:) 1024 bytes.

44) Which of the following is NOT an example of network architecture?

   A) Star
   B) Ring
   C) Bus
   D) Chain
   E) Train

The correct answer is E:) Train.

45) A student learns in a computer class that there are specific protocols for how computers share information over the internet, such as how to transfer information and how to link. The student has learned about

   A) TCP/IP
   B) GUI
   C) HTML
   D) VPN
   E) WAN

The correct answer is A:) TCP/IP. This stands for Transmission Control Protocol/Internet Protocol, and was developed by the Department of Defense.

46) When data is transmitted at very high speeds by using circuits that synchronize data transfer with electronic clock signals it is called

   A) Asynchronous
   B) Synchronous
   C) Full-duplex
   D) Echoplex
   E) Parallel

The correct answer is B:) Synchronous.

47) For which of the following would a mail merge NOT be used?

   A) A magazine company addressing magazines to their subscribers.
   B) A college sending out acceptance letters to their future students.
   C) A high school mailing a monthly newsletter to the parents of the students.
   D) A person writing a personalized note to one of their best friends.
   E) All of the above are situations in which a mail merge could be used.

The correct answer is D:) A person writing a personalized note to one of their best friends. A personalized note would be one of a kind and mail merges are used when there is a large quantity of identical documents with unique traits like names.

48) Also called local echo, this asynchronous transmission can only handle one signal at a time, alternating between two computers

   A) Full-duplex
   B) Half-duplex
   C) Echoplex
   D) Parallel
   E) Modem

The correct answer is B:) Half-duplex.

49) Sound based signals that can be transmitted over the telephone lines

   A) Digital
   B) Modem
   C) Dial tone
   D) Fax
   E) Analog

The correct answer is E:) Analog.

50) A company has many large offices spread out in countries all across the world. They want all of the offices to remain connected, but they determine that a WAN would be too expensive and difficult to maintain. What should they use instead?

   A) LAN
   B) Hub
   C) GUI
   D) VPN
   E) WAN is the only option

The correct answer is D:) VPN. VPNs use private networks, like the internet, to maintain connection. This makes it cheaper and easier than using a WAN.

51) A person sits down at a computer and moves their mouse to click on an icon. The reason they are able to do this is because of

    A) VPN
    B) DSS
    C) HTML
    D) WAN
    E) GUI

The correct answer is E:) GUI. Graphical User Interfaces allow a person to interact with their computer. Before there were GUIs, computers could only be operated through the use of a command line.

52) This occurs when the system is powered on

    A) Cold boot
    B) Warm boot
    C) Reboot
    D) Medium boot
    E) Winter socks

The correct answer is A:) Cold boot.

53) What is the computer equivalent of short-term memory?

    A) A hard drive
    B) LAN
    C) RAM
    D) HTML
    E) OLTP

The correct answer is C:) RAM. Random Access Memory is a short term memory used by computers to avoid the slower hard drive.

54) What connection is used to join a LAN to a WAN?

   A) Bridge
   B) Gateway
   C) Router
   D) Hub
   E) None of the above

The correct answer is B:) Gateway.

55) What connection is used to direct messages through connected networks?

   A) Bridge
   B) Gateway
   C) Router
   D) Hub
   E) None of the above

The correct answer is C:) Router.

56) Which statement is most true about a client/server system?

   A) It is the most common WAN system.
   B) It is more expensive to add to than a multiple-user system.
   C) The server handles all data processing and database management.
   D) Data is stored in a centralized database on the server.
   E) None of the above

The correct answer is D:) Data is stored in a centralized database on the server.

57) Information system attacks are divided into what two types?

   A) Compliant and noncompliant
   B) Internal and external
   C) Foreign and domestic
   D) Malicious and nonmalicious
   E) None of the above

The correct answer is D:) Malicious and nonmalicious.

58) The United States Constitution is

   A) Copyrighted
   B) Public domain
   C) Copyrighted by the public
   D) Officially government property
   E) Subject to mail merging

The correct answer is B:) Public domain. Because it is a government work it is ineligible for copyright and therefore public domain.

59) What is it called when both an old and new system are used simultaneously for conversion to a new system?

   A) Parallel conversion
   B) Phased conversion
   C) Pilot conversion
   D) Plunge
   E) Conversion

The correct answer is A:) Parallel conversion.

60) A student needs to email her thesis paper to her teacher and she knows the file is 12,000 bits. However, she knows that her email carrier will only allow her to attach a certain number of bytes to an email. How many bytes is her paper?

   A) 120
   B) 150
   C) 1200
   D) 1500
   E) 3000

The correct answer is D:) 1500. There are eight bits in one byte. 12,000 bits/8 = 1500 bytes.

61) A handheld computer that is customized for everyday functions for personal organization is called a

    A) PGA
    B) PDA
    C) PC
    D) CPU
    E) POS

The correct answer is B:) PDA.

62) A bank sets up a database through which their users can create online banking accounts and make deposits or withdrawals online in real time. They are able to do this through what type of database?

    A) ERM
    B) OLTP
    C) WAN
    D) VPN
    E) TCP/IP

The correct answer is B:) OLTP. OLTP stands for Online Transaction Processing and allows for real time online transactions.

63) Ergonomics in computing is

    A) The science of programming.
    B) The science of making something easy to use.
    C) The science of seating.
    D) The science of network language.
    E) The science of printing interfaces.

The correct answer is B:) The science of making something easy to use.

64) A group of friends sits in a circle and tries to communicate with each other. They are not allowed to talk, and if they want to send a note to another person they must send it around the circle. This communication is most like a

   A) LAN
   B) WAN
   C) Token ring
   D) Hub
   E) ERM

The correct answer is C:) Token ring. In a token ring, computers are networked in a circle and information must be passed one at a time around the circle.

65) What uses symbols to represent programs or computer functions?

   A) COBOL
   B) BASIC
   C) GUI
   D) JPEG
   E) FORTRAN

The correct answer is C:) GUI.

66) Which of the following resolutions will offer the most clarity?

   A) 50 x 150
   B) 730 x 1000
   C) 840 x 1240
   D) 930 x 1360
   E) 1360 x 1780

The correct answer is E:) 1360 x 1780. The more pixels there are, the higher the resolution. The higher the resolution, the more clear it will be.

67) Which is NOT a procedural programming language?

   A) FORTRAN
   B) BASIC
   C) COBOL
   D) C Language
   E) Java

The correct answer is E:) Java.

68) This software package supports production of documents

   A) Data management software
   B) Word processing
   C) Desktop publishing
   D) Graphics software
   E) Speech recognition software

The correct answer is B:) Word processing.

69) Which of the following was developed to allow designers to determine the look of the web page, and keep the design and content of a web page separate?

   A) ERM
   B) OLTP
   C) HTML
   D) CSS
   E) VPN

The correct answer is D:) CSS.

70) This software incorporates photographs, diagrams and other images with text to produce sophisticated documents

   A) Data management software
   B) Word processing
   C) Desktop publishing
   D) Graphics software
   E) Speech recognition software

The correct answer is C:) Desktop publishing.

71) A manager purchases software to help analyze customer trends. This software is called

   A) CSS
   B) ERM
   C) DSS
   D) VPN
   E) OLTP

The correct answer is B:) ERM. This stands for Enterprise Resource Management.

72) This software provides real-time transcription of voice

   A) Data management software
   B) Word processing
   C) Desktop publishing
   D) Graphics software
   E) Speech recognition software

The correct answer is E:) Speech recognition software.

73) After its creation, ASCII later developed into

   A) CIO
   B) Unicode
   C) HTML
   D) CSS
   E) None of the above

The correct answer is B:) Unicode.

74) Which of the following correctly lists the eight steps of software development?

   A) Requirements definition, requirements analysis, preliminary design, detailed design, implementation, system testing, acceptance testing and maintenance.
   B) Preliminary design, requirements definition, requirements analysis, detailed design, implementation, system testing, acceptance testing and maintenance.
   C) Requirements definition, preliminary design, requirements analysis, detailed design, implementation, acceptance testing, maintenance and system testing.
   D) Requirements analysis, requirements definition, preliminary design, system testing, acceptance testing, implementation and maintenance.
   E) Requirements definition, requirements analysis, preliminary design, detailed design, system testing, acceptance testing and maintenance.

The correct answer is A:) Requirements definition, requirements analysis, preliminary design, detailed design, implementation, system testing, acceptance testing and maintenance.

75) This software allows the user to convert data to a graphical form

   A) Data management software
   B) Word processing
   C) Desktop publishing
   D) Graphics software
   E) Speech recognition software

The correct answer is D:) Graphics software.

76) Whose job is it to recognize the need for, and implement, new technology in a workplace?

   A) CIO
   B) CEO
   C) Project manager
   D) System analyst
   E) None of the above

The correct answer is A:) CIO. CIO stands for Chief Information Officer.

77) Which of the following is NOT a database data model

   A) Hierarchical
   B) Network
   C) Relational
   D) Distributed
   E) Query language

The correct answer is E:) Query language.

78) __ is a program that embeds itself into another program and infects a personal computer when the other program runs.

   A) Virus
   B) Trojan
   C) Red pill
   D) Trojan horse
   E) Blue pill

The correct answer is A:) Virus.

79) The cell in the second column and seventh row is called

   A) G2
   B) B7
   C) BG
   D) 2-7
   E) 7-2

The correct answer is B:) B7.

80) Microsoft Excel is an example of what type of program?

   A) Word processing software
   B) Desktop publishing software
   C) Spreadsheet software
   D) Graphics software
   E) Presentation software

The correct answer is C:) Spreadsheet software.

81) Microsoft Word is an example of what type of program?

   A) Word processing software
   B) Desktop publishing software
   C) Spreadsheet software
   D) Graphics software
   E) Presentation software

The correct answer is A:) Word processing software.

82) In which of the following situations would an expert system be LEAST useful?

   A) Diagnosing a disease based on a list of characteristics.
   B) Fixing a problem based on a list of problems.
   C) Performing complex mathematical calculations.
   D) Determining which of two products would be most successful.
   E) In all of the above situations an expert system would be useful.

The correct answer is D:) Determining which of two products would be most successful. This is a case in which human input is necessary for success.

83) Which of the following is the best definition for a mesh configuration?

   A) Each computer in the network is linked to every other computer.
   B) There is a central computer, to which every other computer is linked.
   C) One computer is linked to several other computers. Each of these is linked to another level of computers.
   D) The computers are linked circularly to a single communication channel.
   E) None of the above

The correct answer is A:) Each computer in the network is linked to every other computer.

84) Which of the following is true about a star network configuration?

   A) It is one of the most reliable configurations, as the network can survive if any one computer fails.
   B) Adding new nodes is difficult.
   C) The entire network will fail if the central computer is down.
   D) The nodes are arranged in a circular, central hub.
   E) None of the above

The correct answer is C:) The entire network will fail if the central computer is down.

85) Which configuration is most likely to be used in a local area network?

   A) Ring
   B) Star
   C) Mesh
   D) Hybrid
   E) None of the above

The correct answer is A:) Ring.

86) What are the basic functions of an information system?

   A) Word processing, communications and storage
   B) Input, processing, storage and output
   C) Decision making, security, filing and access
   D) Input, communications, filing and security
   E) None of the above

The correct answer is B:) Input, processing, storage and output.

87) What does the acronym GIGO stand for?

   A) Garbage in, garbage out
   B) Gigabytes incoming, gigabytes outgoing
   C) Get data in, get data out
   D) Gigabyte internalization and gigabyte optimization
   E) None of the above

The correct answer is A:) Garbage in, garbage out.

88) What connection is used to join two LANs?

   A) Bridge
   B) Gateway
   C) Router
   D) Hub
   E) None of the above

The correct answer is A:) Bridge.

89) Adobe InDesign is an example of what type of program?

   A) Word processing software
   B) Desktop publishing software
   C) Spreadsheet software
   D) Graphics software
   E) Presentation software

The correct answer is B:) Desktop publishing software.

90) Adobe Photoshop is an example of what type of program?

   A) Word processing software
   B) Desktop publishing software
   C) Spreadsheet software
   D) Graphics software
   E) Presentation software

The correct answer is D:) Graphics software.

91) A compiler will translate information from one language, called the source language, into another language, called the

   A) Target language
   B) Final language
   C) Expected language
   D) End language
   E) None of the above

The correct answer is A:) Target language. This is the language that the program should end up in.

92) __ provides access to a remote computer for retrieval of files.

   A) FTP
   B) EDI
   C) URL
   D) TCP
   E) TCP/IP

The correct answer is A:) FTP.

93) Creating a specific list of what needs to be accomplished for a project to be completed occurs in which stage of software development?

   A) Requirements analysis
   B) Preliminary design
   C) System testing
   D) Maintenance
   E) Requirements definition

The correct answer is E:) Requirements definition. This is the first phase of software development.

94) When you do the action CTRL+C what happens?

   A) An item is copied
   B) An item is cut
   C) An item is deleted
   D) An item is saved
   E) An item is bolded

The correct answer is A:) An item is copied.

95) When you copy something to the clipboard, it will remain there until

   A) It is pasted
   B) It is sorted
   C) It is replaced
   D) It is collated
   E) It is bolded

The correct answer is C:) It is replaced.

96) Order the following according to storage capacity: DVD, CD, Blu ray.

   A) CD, DVD, Blu ray
   B) DVD, Blu ray, CD
   C) Blu ray, CD, DVD
   D) DVD, CD, Blu ray
   E) CD, Blu ray, DVD

The correct answer is A:) CD, DVD, Blu ray.

97) Which type of software is free for the public to download and use?

   A) Public-domain software
   B) Shareware
   C) Freeware
   D) Peer-to-peer
   E) Beta software

The correct answer is A:) Public-domain software.

98) Someone who appears legitimate but is in fact soliciting financial information from you or your passwords is called a

   A) Sniffer
   B) Phisher
   C) Tracker
   D) Caster
   E) Mummy

The correct answer is B:) Phisher.

99) Which of the following is NOT a benefit of expert systems?

   A) They can be reproduced quickly and easily.
   B) They are designed to be able to learn.
   C) They can think innovatively and creatively.
   D) They are designed to give explanations to answers determined through a logical process.
   E) They are designed to work like the human brain, efficiently and accurately.

The correct answer is C:) They can think innovatively and creatively. Expert systems must operate through formulaic approaches.

100) Which job function installs and monitors LANs?

   A) Project manager
   B) Software engineer
   C) Network administrator
   D) Data analyst
   E) Beta tester

The correct answer is C:) Network administrator.

101) Approximately how fast do radio waves travel?

   A) 3 m/s
   B) 300 m/s
   C) 300 thousand m/s
   D) 3 million m/s
   E) 300 million m/s

The correct answer is E:) 300 million m/s. This is the speed of light.

102) A person wishes to copy an image from a piece of paper onto a computer. They would need to use a(n)

   A) Scanner
   B) Output device
   C) Fax machine
   D) Printer
   E) None of the above

The correct answer is A:) Scanner. A scanner is an input device. It is used to get an image from paper to the computer screen.

103) Which of the following is another name for a website address?

   A) WAN
   B) ISP
   C) IP address
   D) URL
   E) None of the above

The correct answer is D:) URL. WAN is a Wireless Area Network, ISP is an Internet Service Provider, and IP address is the computer's "address," not the website's.

104) A fax machine sends information

   A) Over the internet
   B) Through a telephone wire
   C) Via satellite
   D) Any of the above
   E) None of the above

The correct answer is B:) Through a telephone wire.

105) Which of the following titles would NOT indicate an image file?

   A) JPEG
   B) GIF
   C) PNG
   D) BIF
   E) None of the above

The correct answer is D:) BIF. These are Boot Information Files.

106) Which type of image file is most used in pictures because of its ability to display smooth color transitions?

   A) JPEG
   B) MPEG
   C) GIF
   D) PNG
   E) None of the above

The correct answer is A:) JPEG. GIF and PNG are high contrast, and MPEGs are used in video.

107) Which of the following charges a periodic fee?

   A) URL
   B) IP
   C) ISP
   D) TCP
   E) None of the above

The correct answer is C:) ISP. The other three answers all relate to the internet, but only Internet Service Provider charges a fee.

108) What can internet users use to find web pages for which they don't know the address?

   A) Uniform resource locator
   B) ISP
   C) Search engine
   D) Database
   E) None of the above

The correct answer is C:) Search engine. A URL would be used if they already knew the address.

109) Which of these is an object-oriented programming language?

   A) FORTRAN
   B) C-Sharp
   C) BASIC
   D) Pascal
   E) None of the above

The correct answer is B:) C-Sharp.

110) Which programming language is the following most likely a sample of?

   10   INPUT NAME$;
   20   PRINT "Hello, " NAME$;

   A) FORTRAN
   B) C-Sharp
   C) BASIC
   D) Pascal
   E) None of the above

The correct answer is C:) BASIC.

111) What is the name of the program that runs the entire time a computer is on?

   A) The processing unit
   B) The supervisor
   C) The logical control program
   D) The arithmetic-logic unit
   E) None of the above

The correct answer is B:) The supervisor.

112) What is the main difference between a bus network and a ring network?

   A) A bus network is linear. A ring network is a loop.
   B) A bus network connects all nodes to a central bus. A ring network connects the nodes directly to each other.
   C) A bus network is more reliable than a ring network.
   D) A bus network is connected to a central computer ("server"). A ring network is a peer-to-peer network.
   E) None of the above

The correct answer is A:) A bus network is linear. A ring network is a loop.

113) Which of the following correctly orders the steps which the CPU follows in executing a command?

   A) Fetch, execute, decode, writeback
   B) Fetch, decode, execute, writeback
   C) Fetch, writeback, execute, decode
   D) Decode, writeback, execute, fetch
   E) None of the above

The correct answer is B:) Fetch, decode, execute, writeback.

114) ARPANET developed

   A) HTTP protocols for transmitting data.
   B) Packet switching for efficiency when transferring data.
   C) Implementing antivirus software and firewalls.
   D) All of the above
   E) None of the above

The correct answer is B:) Packet switching for efficiency when transferring data.

115) Which of the following is NOT a classification of hardware?

   A) Input device
   B) Motherboard
   C) Output device
   D) Storage device
   E) None of the above

The correct answer is B:) Motherboard. The motherboard is a piece of hardware, but it is not a classification of hardware.

116) What was the first functional computer in the United States?

   A) UNIVAC
   B) ENIAC
   C) Atanasoff-Berry computer
   D) Abacus
   E) None of the above

The correct answer is C:) Atanasoff-Berry computer. It was followed by the ENIAC and then UNIVAC a short time after.

117) A person sends an e-mail and makes it appear as though it were coming from someone else. This is called

   A) Hacking
   B) Pharming
   C) Spoofing
   D) Phishing
   E) None of the above

The correct answer is C:) Spoofing. Spoofing is when a person alters or obscures their identity.

118) Which of the following statements is FALSE?

A virus generally requires human action to spread.
A virus can be harmless or malicious.
A virus attaches itself to e-mails only.

   A) I and III only
   B) II only
   C) II and III only
   D) III only
   E) None of the above

The correct answer is D:) III only. A virus attaches itself to files, not just e-mails.

119) Which of the following is NOT a rule of proper netiquette?

   A) Title e-mails with descriptive subjects.
   B) Never type in all capitals.
   C) Always read messages before forwarding.
   D) Never use emoticons.
   E) None of the above

The correct answer is D:) Never use emoticons. Emoticons are allowed, as long as they aren't overused.

120) Which of the following is used to interrogate the databse and retrieve groups of records for analysis?

   A) HTML
   B) PHP
   C) SQL
   D) SKYPE
   E) None of the above

The correct answer is C:) SQL. SQL stands for structured query language.

121) Pseudocode is a

   A) Number code composed of zeros and ones
   B) Method used in Java procedure
   C) Simplified informal language used in program design
   D) Text form and source code of a program
   E) Identifier of variables in a program

The correct answer is: C:) Simplified informal language used in program design. Pseudocode is a detailed and readable design tool that helps programmers to develop algorithms and operate principles of a computer program.

122) Syntax error is an error wherein sequence of characters are placed incorrectly in a program while logic error is

   A) An error in text of code
   B) A bug in a program which causes unwanted output
   C) A code not appearing on actual output
   D) An error in graphics used for codes
   E) An error which causes crashing of program

The correct answer is B:) A bug in a program which causes unwanted output. Logic error causes unnecessary behaviors and output in a program due to the bug acquired.

123) A query is an inquiry into the database by means of the SELECT statement. A correct query is used to

   A) Delete unnecessary data from the database
   B) Copy data from one database to another
   C) Edit data within the database according to own liking
   D) Extract data from the database within a format according to the user's demand
   E) Insert data from database according to format

The correct answer is D:) Extract data from the database within a format according to the user's demand. The SELECT statement is the most commonly used of all SQL commands after a database's establishment. The SELECT statement permits you to view data that is stored in the database.

124) To communicate with satellites, distant geostationary satellites use _____, while low orbit satellites are compatible with _____

A) Microwaves, radio waves
B) Electromagnetic waves, microwaves
C) Microwaves, electromagnetic waves
D) Radio waves, microwaves
E) Electromagnetic waves, radio waves

The correct answer is A:) Microwaves, radio waves. Microwaves pass directly through the atmosphere and are fit for communicating with distant geostationary satellites, while radio waves are appropriate for communicating with satellites in low orbit.

Test Taking Strategies

Here are some test-taking strategies that are specific to this test and to other CLEP tests in general:

- Keep your eyes on the time. Pay attention to how much time you have left.
- Read the entire question and read all the answers. Many questions are not as hard to answer as they may seem. Sometimes, a difficult sounding question really only is asking you how to read an accompanying chart. Chart and graph questions are on most CLEP test and should be an easy free point.
- If you don't know the answer immediately, the new computer-based testing lets you mark questions and come back to them later if you have time.
- Read the wording carefully. Some words can give you hints to the right answer. There are no exceptions to an answer when there are words in the question such as "always" "all" or "none". If one of the answer choices includes most or some of the right answers, but not all, then that is not the answer. Here is an example:

The primary colors include all of the following:

Red, Yellow, Blue, Green
Red, Green, Yellow
Red, Orange, Yellow
Red, Yellow, Blue
None of the above

- Although item A includes all the right answers, it also includes an incorrect answer, making it incorrect. If you didn't read it carefully, were in a hurry, or didn't know the material well, you might fall for this.

- Make a guess on a question that you do not know the answer to. There is no penalty for an incorrect answer. Eliminate the answer choices that you know are incorrect. For example, this will let your guess be a 1 in 3 chance instead.

What Your Score Means

Based on your score, you may, or may not, qualify for credit at your specific institution. At University of Phoenix, a score of 50 is passing for full credit. At Utah Valley State College, the score is unpublished, the school will accept credit on a case-by-case basis. Another school, Brigham Young University (BYU) does not accept CLEP credit. To find out what score you need for credit, you need to get that information from your school's website or academic advisor.

You can score between 20 and 80 on any CLEP test. Some exams include percentile ranks. Each correct answer is worth one point. You lose no points for unanswered or incorrect questions.

Test Preparation

How much you need to study depends upon your knowledge of the subject area. This book is much different than the regular CLEP study guides. This book actually teaches you the information that you need to know to pass the test. The book follows the outline of the knowledge and skills required for the subject matter as stated in the regular study guide. It is important to understand all the major concepts that are listed in the table of contents and it is very important to know any words in bold print.

One of the fallacies of other test books is test questions. People assume that the content of the questions are similar to what will be on the test. **That is not the case.** They are only to test your "test taking skills" so for those who know how to read a question carefully, there is not much added value from taking a "fake" test.

To prepare for the test, make a series of goals. Allot a certain amount of time to review the information you have already studied and to learn additional material. Take notes as you study; it will help you to learn the material.

Legal Note

All rights reserved. This Study Guide, Book and Flashcards are protected under US Copyright Law. No part of this book or study guide or flashcards may be reproduced, distributed or stored in a retrieval system, or transmitted in any form or by any means, electronic, mechanical, photocopying, recording, or otherwise, without the prior written permission of the publisher Breely Crush Publishing, LLC. This manual is not supported by or affiliated with the College Board, creators of the CLEP test. CLEP is a registered trademark of the College Entrance Examination Board, which does not endorse this book.

FLASHCARDS

This section contains flashcards for you to use to further your understanding of the material and test yourself on important concepts, names or dates. Read the term or question then flip the page over to check the answer on the back. Keep in mind that this information may not be covered in the text of the study guide. Take your time to study the flashcards, you will need to know and understand these concepts to pass the test.

Hardware	Software
CISC	ALU
Hard drive	RAM
ROM	Input device

Any program that runs on the computer	Anything that makes up the computer like the monitor, etc.
Arithmetic Logic Unit	Complex Instruction Set Computer
Write and read memory	Stores information
Keyboard, mouse	Read Only Memory

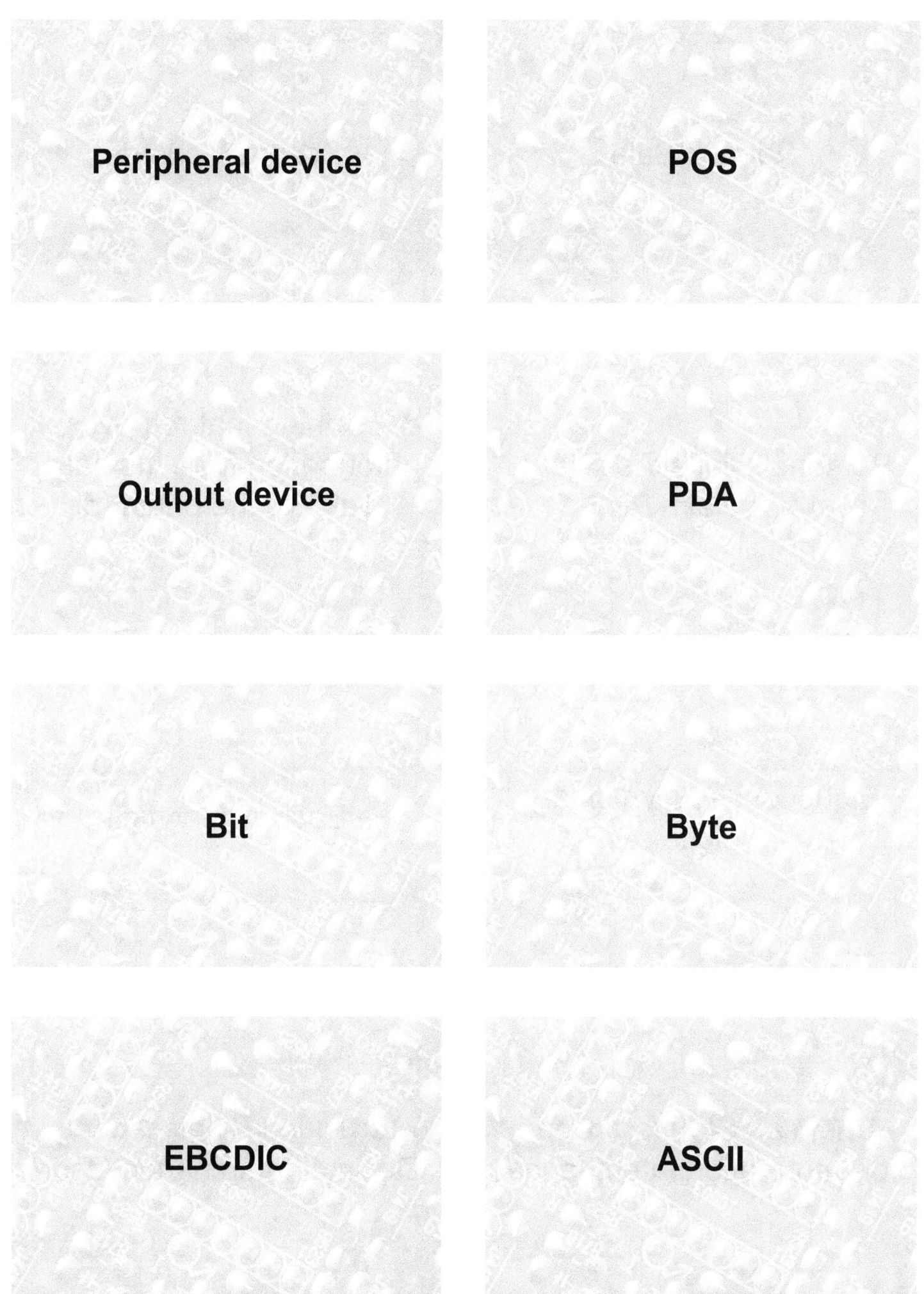

Point of Sale	Scanner, printer
Personal Digital Assistant, ex. a Palm Pilot	Anything that retrieves information from the hard disk like the printer or monitor
Eight consecutive binary digits	Each binary digit
American Standard Code for Information Interchange	Extended Binary Coded Decimal Interchange Code

JPEG	TIFF
MPEG	LAN
Ring network	WAN
Asynchronous	Cold boot

Tagged Image File Format, another type of image file	Image file
Local Area Network	Movie Picture Experts Group, digital video files
Wide Area Network	A network where each node is "daisy chained" to the next node so all connect in a ring
When the system is powered on and restarted by a user	Sending one bit after the other

RAD	**PERT**
Gantt Chart	**Pseudocode**
What are the logical operators?	**Name 2 object-oriented languages**
Name 4 procedural languages	**HTML**

Program Evaluation and Review Technique	Rapid Action Development
Simple and standardized programming language	A chart used in project management which shows the amount of time for each step in the development process
C++, Java	And, or, not
HyperText Markup Language	FORTRAN, BASIC, COBOL, C language

Example of an input device	Peripheral device
Blog	Plunge
SQL	Kilobyte
MHz	Encryption

Any electronic component that is attached to the computer but external to it	Keyboard
Abrupt changeover to a new system without using one of the other conversion techniques first	Online journal or webpage where a person (or company) posts anything they want
1000 bytes	Structured Query Language
Modifying data so that it cannot be deciphered with the encryption key	1 million cycles a second

Firewall	**Storage device**
Application software	**Programming software**
System software	**Graphical User Interface (GUI)**
Slave computer	**Zombie computer**

A classification for hardware which stores information in a computer, such as the hard drive or RAM

A barrier between your computer and other computers. It scans incoming data to be sure it meets security requirements and protects against hackers

A classification for software which is designed to help programmers write programs more effectively and efficiently

A classification for software which is designed to help a computer user accomplish a task

A computer interface which facilitates human and computer interaction through the use of a screen and mouse

A classification for software which runs the computer

A computer which a hacker has taken control of and uses to perform illegal or destructive actions

A computer which a computer owner has networked with another which then controls it

Screen resolution	Uptime
Token ring	Hub
Virtual Private Network (VPN)	Mail merge
Interpreter	Compiler

A measure of the availability of a server	A description of the clarity of a screen based on pixels
A piece of hardware through which computers in a LAN are connected	A network in which computers are linked in a circle and information must be passed one at a time around the circle
A program used to create large amounts of documents which are identical, but have a few unique elements	A private network in which computers are connected through a public network
A program which translates a program written in a computer programming language into machine language	A program which executes instructions in a computer programming language

Java	**Netiquette**
File Transfer Protocol (FTP)	**Antivirus software**
Neural network	**Blu ray**
Radio waves	**MPEG**

A set of guidelines dictating what is or isn't proper to do online	A programming language which is used to create selfcontained programs, called applets, which can be put onto a web page
A software which scans the programs already on the computer for anything dangerous	A set of protocols for transferring files over the internet
A type of disc with higher storage capacity than CDs or DVDs used for high definition videos	A type of artificial intelligence which is designed to work like the human brain
A type of file used for digital videos	A type of electromagnetic wave which is used for satellite transmission

PNG	GIF
Search engine	Online Transaction Processing (OLTP)
Decision Support System (DSS)	ARPANET
Machine language	Expert system

A type of image file used for images with sharp contrasts between colors and which supports simple animations	A type of image file used for images with sharp contrast between colors which does not support animations, but has a larger color range than GIF
A type of program which allows real time online transactions to occur	type of internet search aid used by computer users which finds web pages matching the user's request
A WAN set up by the Department of Defense which played an integral part in the development of internet protocols	A type of software used to help managers or business people to interpret data and make decisions
An application that has been developed using AI methods that have been applied to a highly specific area of knowledge and is capable of giving advice about that area	Also called machine code or binary code. A language created entirely using zeros and ones which is the language computers understand

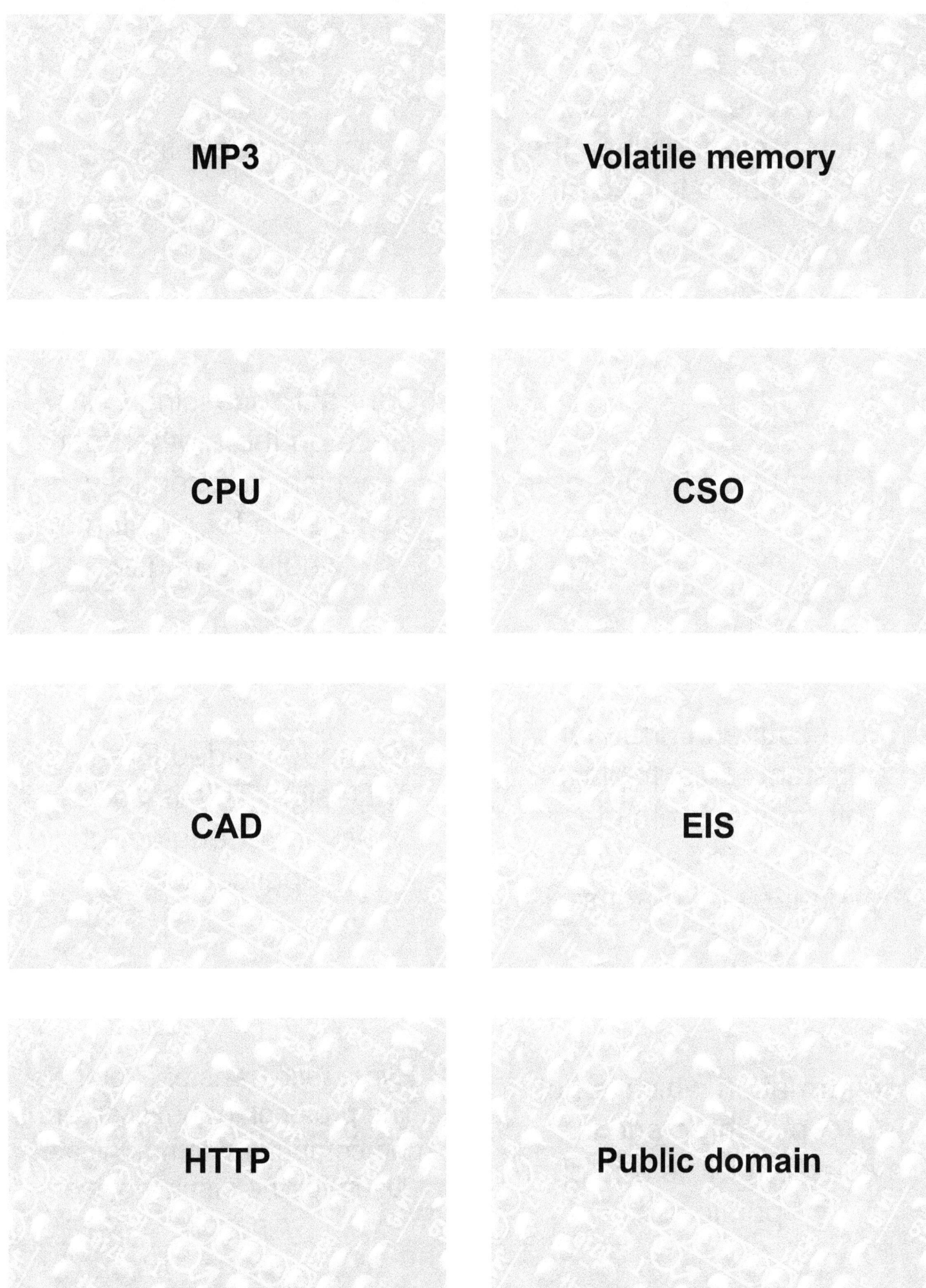

Any type of memory which is erased when the computer is turned off	An audio file
Chief Security Officer	Central Processing Unit. A piece on the motherboard which is essentially responsible for running the whole computer
Executive Information System. This displays information from other databases in easy to read charts and graphs.	Computer Aided Drafting or Design. This is used in software or engineering applications.
Information which is not copyrighted and is available for free and open public use	HyperText Transfer Protocol. The protocol for how servers and computers communicate. Used for the display of web pages

ISP	**Charles Babbage**
OIS	**Pharming**
Cascading Style Sheets (CSS)	**Random Access Memory (RAM)**
Packets	**Cell**

Known as the "father of computing" he was the first person to attempt to build a computation machine	Internet Service Provider. Any company which offers internet access in exchange for a periodic fee.
Pharming is when a hacker makes it so that when you try to go to a website it is secretly redirected to another fake website.	Office Information System
Short term, volatile memory used by computers to avoid the slower hard drive	Programs which allow web designers to more easily manipulate and control the appearance of a web page
The area where a row and column in a spreadsheet intersect	Small units of information which are used in transferring data over the internet

Pipelining	Pixel
Downtime	TCP/IP
URL	Outsourcing
Phishing	Spoofing

The smallest identifiable element which composes the images on a computer screen	The process through which a CPU is able to work on multiple tasks simultaneously
Transmission Control Protocol/Internet Protocol	This is when the server or system is unavailable due to a crash or maintenance
When a company moves part of their business to another location, generally in another country.	Uniform Resource Locator. The website address
When a person alters or obscures their identity online	When a hacker sends an email which leads people to a site which looks legitimate and asks them to enter personal information

www.ingramcontent.com/pod-product-compliance
Lightning Source LLC
Chambersburg PA
CBHW081830300426
44116CB00014B/2542